# Revision

# Framework

# MATHS

# National Curriculum Levels 6-8

David Capewell
Jayne Kranat
Peter Mullarkey

## OXFORD
### UNIVERSITY PRESS

# OXFORD
UNIVERSITY PRESS

Great Clarendon Street, Oxford OX2 6DP

Oxford University Press is a department of the University of Oxford.
It furthers the University's objective of excellence in research,
scholarship, and education by publishing worldwide in

Oxford  New York

Auckland  Cape Town  Dar es Salaam  Hong Kong  Karachi
Kuala Lumpur  Madrid  Melbourne  Mexico City  Nairobi
New Delhi  Shanghai  Taipei  Tokyo  Toronto

With offices in

Argentina  Austria  Brazil  Chile  Czech Republic  France  Greece
Guatemala  Hungary  Italy  Japan  South Korea  Poland  Portugal
Singapore  Switzerland  Thailand  Turkey  Ukraine  Vietnam

First published 2004

British Library Cataloguing in Publication Data

Data available

ISBN 019 914945 3

10 9 8 7 6 5 4 3 2 1

Typeset by Mathematical Composition Setters Ltd.

Printed and bound in Spain by Unigraf S.L.

## Acknowledgements

The publisher would like to thank QCA for their kind permission to use
Key Stage 3 test questions.

# About this book

This book has been written to help you revise for the National Tests at the end of KS3 Mathematics and is aimed at the 6–8 tier of entry.

The books consists of three types of pages:
▷ Contents pages that set out the information you need to know and provide practice
▷ Revision pages that consist of past paper test questions
▷ Practice test paper pages that provide confidence for the real thing.

The **Content** pages are organised into Number (N), Algebra (A), Shape, space and measure (S) and Data handling (D).

They tell you the main ideas you need to know and remember.

Key points tell you the information you need to know.

▶ You can write all numbers in **standard form:**
$A \times 10^n$    where $1 \leqslant A < 10$    and $n$ is an integer.

> You multiply or divide the number by an integer power of 10.

Worked examples show the skills you need in the tests, and margin boxes give you extra hints and tips.

> **example**
> Explain if this statement is true or false. $\frac{1}{a} + \frac{1}{b} = \frac{2}{a+b}$
> ................................................................................................
> $\frac{1}{a} + \frac{1}{b} = \frac{b}{ab} + \frac{a}{ab} = \frac{a+b}{ab}$, so the statement is false.

> See N3 for adding fractions.

The questions give you plenty of practice at specific National Curriculum levels so you can measure your progress against national standards.

## Exercise N2

  **1** What is six cubed?

**2** What is the square of three hundred?

▷  shows a mental test question.

▷ means you can use a calculator.

The **Revision** pages are numbered **R1** to **R6**. These pages are full of past paper Test questions at each of the relevant levels so you experience the style of question you will see in the actual Tests. Each question refers you back to the relevant spread so you can go back over any content you need to practice further.

At the end to the book, there are two **Practice Test Papers** which mirror the style and content of the real thing. If you take these tests under exam conditions you will get a good idea of how you are performing. Do take into account that the actual tests are slightly faster as you can write on them.

All the **Answers** are at the back of the book so you can test yourself.

# Contents

# How to revise using this book

A good way to revise is to start with the Revision pages (**R1** to **R6**) to see what you know and what you need to practise.

Do each one in turn.

Each question refers you back to the content that you need to practise.

To revise a topic:
▶ Read the page through slowly and carefully.
▶ Make sure you understand each step of the worked examples.
▶ Make sure you understand the information in each key point.
▶ Work through the topic questions, as they will help you identify which sorts of questions may cause problems.
▶ Read through the topic again a few days later to help you remember.

Once you are confident you understand the key ideas, set aside an hour and test yourself using Practice Test Paper 1. You can see the equipment you'll need at the start of the test – make sure you have it all ready before you start.

Remember that in the actual test you'll be able to fill in the answers on the sheet so it will take less time. You could allow yourself an extra 15 minutes in the Practice Test Papers for all the copying and filling in you need to do.

Talk to your teacher about any difficulties you have found, then move on to Practice Test Paper 2.

Good luck!

You can round to a given number of **decimal places** or **significant figures**.

**KEYWORDS**
Decimal places          Round
Significant figures
Standard form

▷ To round a number if the first digit not required is 5 or more you round up: 187 is 190 to the nearest 10.
▷ To round to 2 dp (decimal places) you leave 2 digits after the decimal point: 3.8946 is 3.89 to 2 dp.
▷ To round to 3 sf (significant figures) you count 3 digits, starting with the first non-zero digit from the left: 5362 = 5360 and 0.04625 is 0.0463 to 3 sf.

▶ The **upper and lower bounds** of a number are half the rounded amount added to and subtracted from the number.

**example**

Find the upper and lower bounds of these numbers.

**a** 260 has been rounded to the nearest 10
**b** 3.2 has been rounded to the nearest 0.1

...........................................................................

**a** Half of 10 is 5, so upper bound = 260 + 5 = 265, lower bound = 260 − 5 = 255.
**b** Half of 0.1 is 0.05, so upper bound = 3.2 + 0.05 = 3.25, lower bound = 3.2 − 0.05 = 3.15.

Imagine the number line:

3.15          3.25

3.1          3.2          3.3

▶ You can write all numbers in **standard form:**
$A \times 10^n$      where $1 \leqslant A < 10$      and $n$ is an integer.

You multiply or divide the number by an integer power of 10.

For large numbers $n$ is positive, for small numbers $n$ is negative.

**example**

Write these in standard form:   **a** 4 310 000   **b** 0.0037

.............................................................................

**a** $4\ 310\ 000 = 4.31 \times 10^6$

**b** $0.0037 = 3.7 \times 10^{-3}$

You can only add or subtract numbers in standard form if the numbers have the same value of $n$ in $A \times 10^n$.

See N7 to use a calculator with numbers given in standard form.

**example**

Find the difference between $7.4 \times 10^5$ and $6 \times 10^3$.

.............................................................................

First make the powers of 10 the same:

You may need to write your answer in standard form.

$$7.4 \times 10^5 = 740 \times 10^3$$
$$740 \times 10^3 - 6 \times 10^3 = (740 - 6) \times 10^3$$
$$= 736 \times 10^3$$
$$= 7.36 \times 10^5$$

# Exercise N1

**L6** 🔢 **1** There were 78 400 people at a football match.
Nearly 30% were children.

    **a** The percentage was rounded to the nearest whole number, 30.
      What is the smallest value that the percentage could have been, to one decimal place?
    **b** What is the smallest number of children that there might have been at the football match?
      (Use your answer to part **a** to help you).

🔢 **2** 142 students sat an exam. Just over 50% of the students passed.
The percentage was rounded to the nearest whole number.

    **a** What is the largest value that the percentage could have been, to 1 decimal place?
    **b** What is the largest number of students that passed the exam?
      (Use your answer to part **a** to help you).

**L7** **3** In a high jump competition, a distance jumped was recorded as 1.47 m to the nearest centimetre.
Could the distance jumped have been higher than 1.47 m? Explain your answer.

**M** **4** At school sports day the 100 m sprint was won in a time 16.7 seconds measured to the nearest tenth of a second.
Between what two values does this time actually lie?

**M** **5** Joe's height was measured to be 170 cm to the nearest cm.
Between what two values does his height lie?

**6** A sign in the lift reads 'maximum weight 6300 kg'.
This weight is given correct to 2 significant figures.
What is the maximum weight the lift can safely carry?

**L8** **7** Choose from the numbers below one that is the same as $3.9 \times 10^7$.
    $39^7$      $39^6$      $(3.9 \times 10)^7$      $0.39 \times 10^6$      $39 \times 10^6$

**8** What is the difference between $4.6 \times 10^5$ cm and $4.6 \times 10^5$ mm?
Give your answer in standard form.

🔢 **9** The speed of sound is $7.5 \times 10^2$ miles per hour.
What is the speed of sound in miles per second?
Give your answer in standard form.

**M** **10** The diameter of the Sun is 865 000 miles.
Write this number in standard form.

**11** The diameter of the Earth is $1.3 \times 10^4$ km.
The diameter of the Moon is $3.5 \times 10^3$ km.
How many times smaller is the diameter of the Moon than the diameter of the Earth?

**12** $\frac{1}{20\,000} = 0.000\,05$
    **a** Write $0.000\,05$ in standard form.
    **b** Write $\frac{1}{200\,000}$ in standard form.
    **c** Work out $\frac{1}{20\,000} + \frac{1}{200\,000}$. Give your answer in standard form.

**13** Two parcels were weighed to be 12 kg and 17 kg.
Each weight is correct to the nearest kg.
What is the maximum difference in the weight of these two parcels?

🔢 **14** Work out $(4.6 \times 10^{12}) \times (3.1 \times 10^9)$.
Give your answer in standard form.

🔢 **15** Work out $(6.05 \times 10^8) \times (2.5 \times 10^7)$.
Give your answer in standard form.

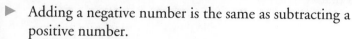

▶ Adding a negative number is the same as subtracting a positive number.
▶ Subtracting a negative number is the same as adding a positive number.

**example**

Work out: **a** $17 + {}^-4$ **b** $9 - {}^-2$ **c** ${}^-3 + {}^-5$ **d** ${}^-11 - {}^-6$

**a** $17 + {}^-4 = 17 - 4 = 13$      **b** $9 - {}^-2 = 9 + 2 = 11$
**c** ${}^-3 + {}^-5 = {}^-3 - 5 = {}^-8$      **d** ${}^-11 - {}^-6 = {}^-11 + 6 = {}^-5$

A **negative number** is a number less than zero.

▶ A **prime** number has two different factors, the number itself and 1.
▶ A **prime factor** is a factor that is also a prime number.

A factor of a number will divide exactly into that number.

You can write a number as a product of its prime factors.
For example, 110 written as a product of its prime factors is $2 \times 5 \times 11$.

▶ The **triangle numbers** form the sequence **1, 3, 6, 10, 15, 21, 28, ...**

The difference between triangle numbers increases by one each time.

▶ The **square numbers** are the result of multiplying a number by itself.
$1 \times 1 = \mathbf{1}$, $2 \times 2 = \mathbf{4}$, $3 \times 3 = \mathbf{9}$, $4 \times 4 = \mathbf{16}$, $5 \times 5 = \mathbf{25}$, ...

▶ A **power** or **index** shows the number of times a number is multiplied by itself.
$4^5$ means $4 \times 4 \times 4 \times 4 \times 4$ (4 to the power 5)

$1^3, 2^3, 3^3, 4^3, ...$ are cube numbers.

▶ A **root** of a number is the reverse of a power.
▷ The square root ($\sqrt{\phantom{x}}$) of a number is the opposite of squaring.
$\sqrt{64} = 8$      ($8 \times 8 = 64$)
▷ The cube root ($\sqrt[3]{\phantom{x}}$) of a number is the opposite of cubing.
$\sqrt[3]{64} = 4$      ($4 \times 4 \times 4 = 64$)

You can use these rules to multiply and divide powers of the same numbers.

To use these rules the base number has to be the same, for example:
$3^2 \times 3^4 = 3^{2+4} = 3^6$

▶ When you multiply, add the powers.
▶ When you divide, subtract the powers.

**example**

Work out:
**a** $4^3 \times 4^5$ **b** $7^9 \div 7^4$
**c** $(2 \times 10^5) \times (4 \times 10^7)$
**d** $(7.2 \times 10^8) \div (3 \times 10^2)$

**a** $4^3 \times 4^5 = 4^{3+5} = 4^8$
**b** $7^9 \div 7^4 = 7^{9-4} = 7^5$
**c** $(2 \times 10^5) \times (4 \times 10^7) = (2 \times 4) \times 10^{5+7} = 8 \times 10^{12}$
**d** $(7.2 \times 10^8) \div (3 \times 10^2) = (7.2 \div 3) \times 10^{8-2} = 2.4 \times 10^6$

When you calculate the power of a number it will get much bigger or much smaller quite quickly, for example:

Powers of 3: $3^2 = 9$, $3^3 = 27$, $3^4 = 81$, $3^5 = 243$, $3^6 = 729$, $3^7 = 2187$
Powers of 0.2: $0.2^2 = 0.04$, $0.2^3 = 0.008$, $0.2^4 = 0.0016$, $0.2^5 = 0.00032$

## Exercise N2

**L6** **M** **1** What is six cubed?

**M** **2** What is the square of three hundred?

**M** **3** What is the square root of eighty-one?

**M** **4** What is the square root of ten thousand?

**M** **5** What is the cube root of sixty-four?

**6** Choose from these numbers: $1^7$    $2^5$    $3^4$    $4^3$    $9^2$

   **a** the smallest number
   **b** a number that is not a square number
   **c** numbers that are equal.

**7** A solid cuboid is made from centimetre cubes. It has a volume of 48 cm$^3$. It is 4 cm high. Write down the possible dimensions of the other sides.

**8**

   **a** Choose the correct card to complete these calculations.
     **i** $^-4 + 2 + \square = 3$    **ii** $+6 - \square = +8$
   **b** Choose a card that gives the lowest possible answer to   $^-3 - \square =$   Complete the sum.
   **c** Choose a card that gives the highest possible answer to   $^-3 - \square =$   Complete the sum.

**L7**    **9** Write the number 72 as a product of prime factors.

**M** **10** Six to the power five multiplied by six to the power seven is equal to six to the power what?

**M** **11** Four to the power eight divided by four to the power two is equal to four to the power what?

**M** **12** What would be the last digit in these quantities?

   **a** nineteen to the power three
   **b** eighty-three to the power seven
   **c** two hundred and thirty-four to the power four

**13** Write down the value of $k$ if $64 = 2^k$.

**14** Write 120 as a product of prime factors.

**M** **15** Nine to the power fifteen divided by nine to the power fourteen is equal to what?

**16** $2^6 = 64$. Work out $2^7$.

**17** $10^6 = 1\,000\,000$. Work out $10^{12}$.

**18** Write down the values of $x$ and $y$ if: $256 = 16^x = 4^y$

**L8** **19** $3^7 = 2187$. Work out $3^6$.

**20**

   $n$ is a positive integer.

   **a** Choose a card that will always give an answer less than $n$.
   **b** When $n = 1$, choose a card or cards that will give an answer of 1.
   **c** When $n$ is less than 1, choose a card or cards that will give an answer less than 1.
   **d** When $n = 2$, choose a card or cards that will give an answer greater than 2.

**21** $6^0 = 1$     $6^1 = 6$     $6^2 = 36$     $6^3 = 216$     $6^4 = 1296$     $6^5 = 7776$     $6^6 = 46\,656$
   Use the values to:     **a** explain why $36 \times 216 = 7776$     **b** work out $\frac{46\,656}{36}$.

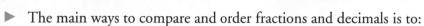

▶ The main ways to compare and order fractions and decimals is to:
  ▷ change them into decimals
  ▷ change them into fractions with the same denominator.

▶ To change a fraction to a decimal divide the numerator by the denominator:
$$\tfrac{3}{8} = 3 \div 8 = 0.375$$

▶ To change a decimal to a percentage multiply by 100:
$0.375 = 37.5\%$     $(0.375 \times 100 = 37.5)$

▶ To change a decimal to a fraction use the number of decimal places it is written to:
| | | |
|---|---|---|
| 0.4 has 1 decimal place | $0.4 = \tfrac{4}{10}$ | (1 zero) |
| 0.23 has 2 decimal places | $0.23 = \tfrac{23}{100}$ | (2 zeros) |
| 0.06 has 2 decimal places | $0.06 = \tfrac{6}{100}$ | (2 zeros) |

Some fractions have decimal equivalents that **recur**.

You should learn:     $\tfrac{1}{3} = 0.\dot{3}$     $\tfrac{2}{3} = 0.\dot{6}$

▶ To add or subtract fractions they must have the same denominator, you then add or subtract the numerators only.

> **example**
>
> Work out:
>
> **a** $\tfrac{2}{5} + \tfrac{3}{8}$   **b** $\tfrac{5}{6} - \tfrac{1}{4}$
>
> **a** Write both fractions with a common denominator and then add the numerators:
> $$\tfrac{2}{5} + \tfrac{3}{8} = \tfrac{16}{40} + \tfrac{15}{40} = \tfrac{31}{40}$$
>
> **b** Write both fractions with a common denominator and then subtract the numerators:
> $$\tfrac{5}{6} - \tfrac{1}{4} = \tfrac{10}{12} - \tfrac{3}{12} = \tfrac{7}{12}$$

▶ To multiply fractions you multiply the numerators and denominators separately.

> **example**
>
> Work out:
>
> **a** $\tfrac{3}{7} \times \tfrac{4}{5}$   **b** $\tfrac{5}{8} \times \tfrac{2}{9}$
>
> **a** $\tfrac{3}{7} \times \tfrac{4}{5} = \tfrac{3 \times 4}{7 \times 5} = \tfrac{12}{35}$     **b** $\tfrac{5}{8} \times \tfrac{2}{9} = \tfrac{5 \times 2}{8 \times 9} = \tfrac{10}{72} = \tfrac{5}{36}$

▶ To divide fractions you turn the second fraction upside-down and change the division to a multiplication:
$$\tfrac{3}{5} \div \tfrac{7}{8} = \tfrac{3}{5} \times \tfrac{8}{7} = \tfrac{3 \times 8}{5 \times 7} = \tfrac{24}{35}$$

**KEYWORDS**
| | |
|---|---|
| Denominator | Numerator |
| Recur | Terminating |
| Decimal places | |

Fractions, decimals and percentages are three ways of writing the same number.

Use this method with terminating decimals.

$0.\dot{3} = 0.333333...$

If you are multiplying or dividing a mixed number then change it to an improper fraction first.

## Exercise N3

**L6**

**1** What is one-sixth of three-fifths of fifty?

**2** Work out:

    **a** $\frac{2}{7} + \frac{5}{14}$     **b** $\frac{7}{11} - \frac{7}{33}$

**3** Which is bigger: 49% or $\frac{4}{9}$? Show your working.

**4** Which is smaller: 27% or $\frac{2}{7}$? Show your working.

**5 a** How many fifths are there in $3\frac{1}{10}$?
  **b** Work out $3\frac{1}{10} \div \frac{7}{10}$.

**L7**

**6**

From these fractions choose:

    **a** two fractions to give the lowest possible answer when multiplied together
    **b** three fractions that add up to 1
    **c** a fraction that has a recurring decimal equivalent.

**7** Choose from this list:     0.4     0.002     4     5     0.1

    **a** two numbers that have the lowest possible product
    **b** two numbers that multiply together to give $\frac{1}{100}$
    **c** two numbers to complete this division: ... ÷ ... = 10.

**8** A unit fraction has numerator 1 and denominator greater than 1,
for example $\frac{1}{4}, \frac{1}{5}, \frac{1}{6}$ are all unit fractions.
All fractions can be written as the sum or difference of unit fractions,
for example $\frac{5}{12} = \frac{1}{4} + \frac{1}{6}$

    **a** What fractions are represented by these?
      **i** $\frac{1}{5} + \frac{1}{8}$     **ii** $\frac{1}{2} - \frac{1}{5}$
    **b** Write these fractions as the sum or difference of unit fractions.
      **i** $\frac{5}{6}$    **ii** $\frac{2}{15}$
    **c** What fraction can be written as the sum $\frac{1}{3} + \frac{1}{4}$?
    **d** Write $\frac{8}{15}$ as the sum of two unit fractions (one of the fractions is $\frac{1}{3}$).
    **e** Write $\frac{11}{28}$ as the sum of two unit fractions.

**9** Choose from this list:
    0.01    0.2    0.8    2.5    4    5

    **a** Which two decimals give the lowest possible product?     .... × .... = ....
    **b** Which two decimals give the answer 20?           .... ÷ .... = 20

**L8**

**10** Work out:

    **a** $\frac{2}{7} \times \frac{9}{16}$     **b** $2\frac{1}{3} \times \frac{3}{5}$     **c** $1\frac{5}{6} \times 3\frac{3}{4}$

**11** Work out:

    **a** $\frac{3}{8} \div \frac{6}{7}$     **b** $\frac{4}{9} \div \frac{3}{4}$     **c** $1\frac{1}{2} \div \frac{2}{5}$

**12** Work out:

    **a** $2\frac{1}{4} \times \frac{3}{5}$     **b** $1\frac{5}{6} \times \frac{4}{11}$     **c** $\frac{2}{3} \times 1\frac{1}{4}$

**13** Work out:

    **a** $1\frac{1}{2} \div \frac{2}{5}$     **b** $2\frac{3}{4} \div \frac{5}{6}$

You can use a multiplier to increase or decrease by a percentage.

KEYWORDS
Percentage          Ratio
Increase            Proportion
Decrease

**example**

**a**  Increase £56 by 15%.   **b**  Decrease £68 by 6%.

**a**  100% + 15% = 115%, as a decimal 115% = 1.15 (this is the multiplier)
56 × 1.15 = £64.40
**b**  100% − 6% = 94%, as a decimal 94% = 0.94 (this is the multiplier)
68 × 0.94 = £63.92

You could be asked to find an amount before an increase or decrease by a percentage.

**example**

**a**  The price of a dress was £42 after a reduction of 20%. Find the original price.
**b**  A telephone bill of £75.20 included VAT at 17.5%. How much was the bill without VAT?

**a**  £42 represents 80% (100 − 20)
Original price = 42 ÷ 0.8 = £52.50
**b**  £75.20 represents 117.5% (100 + 17.5)
Bill less VAT = 75.2 ÷ 1.175 = £64

You divide by the multiplier to get back to the original price.

▶  A **ratio** compares the size of one part with the size of another part.

You can use a ratio when things are in proportion.

**example**

These triangles are similar. Find $x$.

 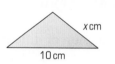

The ratio of the sides is the same so $\frac{5}{8} = \frac{x}{10}$.
This gives $x = \frac{5}{8} \times 10 = 6.25$ cm.

▶  To share an amount in a ratio 3 : 5, divide the original amount by 8 (3 + 5), then multiply the answer by 3 for the first share and by 5 for the second share.

**example**

Share £48 in the ratio 1 : 2 : 3.

The total number of parts = 1 + 2 + 3 = 6. So each part is worth £48 ÷ 6 = £8.
£8 × 2 = £16 and £8 × 3 = £24, so £48 shared in the ratio 1 : 2 : 3 is £8, £16 and £24.

Sometimes it is easier to use a unit ratio.

**example**

A 160 g cereal bar has 220 calories. Find the number of calories in 100 g of the cereal bar.

160 g : 220 calories, dividing both sides of the ratio by 160 gives
1 g : 1.375 calories.
Multiplying both sides by 100 then gives 100 g : 137.5 calories.
So there are 137.5 calories in 100 g of the cereal bar.

To find a unit ratio, divide both numbers by the smallest number.

## Exercise N4

L6  **1** Share:

  **a** £60 in the ratio 1 : 4     **b** £108 in the ratio 5 : 3.

 **2** In a 400 g tin of salmon there are 250 calories.
How many calories are there in a 125 g serving?

**3** Joshua is 12 years old. Reuben is exactly 3 years younger, so Reuben is 9 years old.
The ratio of their ages is 12 : 9, written as simply as possible the ratio is 4 : 3.

  **a** When Joshua is 15 years old, what will be the ratio of Joshua's age to Reuben's age?
  Write this ratio as simply as possible.

  **b** When Reuben is 15 years old, what will be the ratio of Joshua's age to Reuben's age?

  **c** How old were they when the ratio of Joshua's age to Reuben's age was 2 : 1?

 **4** The table shows the numbers of different ices sold and
the amount of money taken at a show one evening.

  **a** What percentage of the total ices sold were cornets?

  **b** What percentage of the total takings were for
  cornets?

  **c** Which type of ice is the most expensive, cornet or tub?
  Explain how you found your answer.

| Ice-cream | Choc-ice | Cornet | Tub | Total |
|---|---|---|---|---|
| Number sold | 60 | 150 | 90 | 300 |
| Amount taken | £60 | £180 | £135 | £370 |

**5** On a farm 40 cows gave birth. 30% of the cows gave birth to two calves.
The rest of the cows gave birth to one calf each.
In total how many calves were born?

L7 **6** Copy and complete the following.

  **a** To increase an amount by 53% multiply by ..................

  **b** To decrease an amount by 21% multiply by ..................

 **7 a** Increase £42 by 16%.     **b** Decrease £42 by 15%.

 **8** Mrs Brown borrows £600.
There are two ways in which she can borrow the money:

  **i** at an interest rate of 5% for five years

  **ii** at an interest rate of 8% for 3 years.

  Which option involves paying less interest and by how much?

 **9** In a shoe shop sale the price of a pair of shoes was reduced by 10% for each day of the sale.
On the Monday of the sale the price of a pair of shoes was £45.

  **a** How much would you have to pay if you bought these shoes on the Thursday?

  **b** How many days would it take before the shoes cost less than £25?

  **c** Explain why the price of the shoes would never be reduced to nothing.

L8  **10** A girls' school has a mixed sixth form. The ratio of boys to girls at the school is 1 : 24. There are
1725 pupils at the school. How many of the pupils are boys?

**11 a** One calculation below gives the answer to: 42 increased by 7%.
  Choose the correct calculation.

  42 × 0.07     42 × 0.7     42 × 1.07     42 × 1.7

  **b** For each of the other calculations, write down a question about percentages that the
  calculation could represent.

**12** Copy and complete this sentence with a decimal number:
'To decrease 42 by 7% multiply 42 by ...'

 **13** A 7% increase followed by another 7% increase is not the same as a total percentage increase of 14%.
What is the total percentage increase? Show your working.

 **14** In a sale, prices were reduced by 20%. The sale price of a T-shirt is £25.60.
What was the price of the T-shirt before the sale?

You can use known facts to perform difficult calculations.

KEYWORDS
Partitioning          Compensating

**example**

Given that $430 \times 5.8 = 2494$, find:

**a** $43\,000 \times 58$  **b** $0.43 \times 58$  **c** $24\,940 \div 43$

**a** $43\,000$ is 100 times bigger, 58 is 10 times bigger, so answer is 1000 times bigger: $43\,000 \times 58 = 2\,494\,000$

**b** $0.43$ is 1000 times smaller, 58 is 10 times bigger so answer is 100 times smaller: $0.43 \times 58 = 24.94$

**c** $24\,940 = 10 \times 2494$, $43 = 430 \div 10$, so answer is 100 times bigger: $24\,940 \div 43 = 580$

Always use rounding to check that the order of your answer is correct.

Use fractions:
$$\frac{2494 \times 10}{430 \div 10} = \frac{2494 \times 10}{430 \times \frac{1}{10}}$$
$$= \frac{2494 \times 10 \times 10}{430}$$

You can use doubling and halving.

**example**

Find:  **a** $17.5\%$ of 92  **b** $22\%$ of 86.

**a** $10\%$ of $92 = 9.2$, so $5\%$ is $4.6$ ($\frac{1}{2}$ of 9.2) and $2.5\%$ is $2.3$ ($\frac{1}{2}$ of 4.6)
$17.5\%$ is $10\% + 5\% + 2.5\%$, $9.2 + 4.6 + 2.3 = 16.1$

**b** $10\%$ of $86 = 8.6$, so $1\%$ is $0.86$, so $11\% = 9.46$ ($8.6 + 0.86$)
Double to get $22\%$: $9.46 \times 2 = 18.92$

You can use partitioning and compensating.

**example**

**a** Find the time difference between 9.47 am and 1.14 pm.
**b** Calculate $12.71 - 8.86$.
**c** Calculate $49 \times 372$.

**a** Split up the time line.
13 minutes to 10 am, 3 hours to 1 pm, plus 14 minutes
Total time = 3 hours 27 minutes

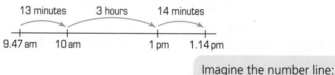

**b** Round up and compensate:
$12.71 - 9 + 0.14 = 3.71 + 0.14 = 3.85$

**c** $49$ is near 50 and 50 is $\frac{1}{2}$ of 100 so calculate $50 \times 372 = \frac{1}{2}$ of $37\,200 = 18\,600$.
$49$ is 1 less than 50 so subtract 372: $49 \times 372 = 18\,600 - 372 = 18\,228$

Imagine the number line:

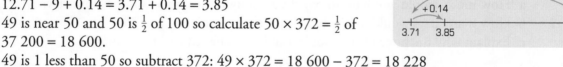

▶ You can simplify fractions by cancelling common factors.

**example**

Find:  **a** $\frac{4}{27} \times \frac{6}{11}$  **b** $17\%$ of £80 000.

**a** $\frac{4}{{}_{9}\cancel{27}} \times \frac{\cancel{6}^{2}}{11} = \frac{4}{9} \times \frac{2}{11} = \frac{8}{99}$

**b** $\frac{17}{100} \times 80\,000 = 17 \times 80 = 1360$

You can change between fractions, decimals and percentages to make it easier to calculate:
$17\% = \frac{17}{100}$

## Exercise N5

In this exercise remember to write down enough working to show that you haven't used a calculator.

**L6**

**1** A desert town gets on average three point three millimetres of rain per year. How much rain could this town expect to get over thirty years?

**M** **2** Work out the answer to these:

  **a** nine point six divided by two
  **b** seventy point two divided by three.

**3** Jenny's hand span is 9.8 cm.
Mark's hand span is 10% greater. What is Mark's hand span?

**M** **4** What is nought point six divided by nought point nought one?

**M** **5** What is nought point five three divided by nought point one?

**M** **6** Look at this calculation: $442 \div 17 = 26$
What is four hundred and forty-two divided by one point seven?

**M** **7** How many nought point two's are there in fourteen?

**L7**

**8** Given that $36.9 \times 5.8 = 214.02$, find:

  **a** $369 \times 58$    **b** $0.369 \times 5.8$    **c** $3.69 \times 580$    **d** $21\,402 \div 36.9$

**9** Show how you can increase 485 by 19%.
Write down your answer.

**10** A restaurant adds 17.5% to its bills.
Write down a method you could use without a calculator to add 17.5% to a bill.
Use your method to work out £56.80 plus 17.5%.

**M** **11** Look at this calculation: $13 \times 48 = 624$
What is six hundred and twenty-four divided by one point three?

**M** **12** Look at this calculation: $576 \div 32 = 18$
What is five hundred and seventy-six divided by one point eight?

**L8**

**13** Choose your answers from this list:
$0.5$    $0.5^2$    $0.5^3$    $\frac{1}{0.5}$    $\frac{1}{0.5^2}$

  **a** Which is the smallest number? Explain how you know.
  **b** Which is the largest number? Explain how you know.

**14** Which of the following are true?

  **a** $\sqrt{0.1} < 0.1$    **b** $\sqrt{0.1} = 0.1$    **c** $\sqrt{0.1} > 0.1$
  Explain how you know.

**15** Put the following in order of size, smallest first.
$0.05$    $\frac{1}{0.05}$    $\sqrt{0.05}$    $0.05^2$

**16** Which of these statements is true?
  A  $3 \times 10^5$ is greater than $3^5$
  B  $3 \times 10^5$ is the same as $3^5$
  C  $3 \times 10^5$ is smaller than $3^5$
  Explain your answer.

**17** A 50% increase followed by another 50% increase is not the same as an increase of 100%.
What is the total percentage increase?
Show your working.

When you add or subtract decimals keep the decimal points underneath each other.

**example**

Work out:   **a** $64 - 0.98$   **b** $203.87 + 7.2009$

**a**
$$\begin{array}{r} 64 \\ -\ \ 0.98 \\ \hline 63.02 \end{array}$$

**b**
$$\begin{array}{r} 203.87 \\ +\ \ 7.2009 \\ \hline 211.0709 \end{array}$$

**KEYWORDS**
Brackets          Of
Multiply          Divide
Add               Subtract
Power             Estimate

Always estimate calculations by rounding.

When you multiply with decimals you can use an equivalent calculation. The answer will have the same number of places after the decimal point as there are in total in the question.

If there is no decimal point shown it will be after the last digit.

A zero at the end of a number will count as one of the places.

**example**

Work out:   **a** $4.2 \times 0.006$   **b** $0.008 \times 0.03$   **c** $0.056 \times 0.5$

**a**   $42 \times 6 = 256$
so $4.2 \times 0.006 = 0.0256$

**b**   $8 \times 3 = 24$
so $0.008 \times 0.03 = 0.000\ 24$

**c**   $56 \times 5 = 280$
so $0.056 \times 0.05 = 0.0028$

To divide with decimals, multiply both numbers by the same power of 10 to get a division by an integer.

**example**

Work out:   **a** $0.975 \div 0.03$   **b** $672 \div 1.6$

**a**   Multiply both numbers by 100:
**b**   Multiply both numbers by 10:
$97.5 \div 3 = 32.5$          $6720 \div 16 = 420$

You need to use the correct order of operations to work out a calculation.

**example**

Calculate $\frac{(4.2 - 1.7)^2}{10} + \frac{19.1 \times 3}{\sqrt{12 \times 3}}$.

First work out the **brackets**:          $\frac{2.5^2}{10} + \frac{19.1 \times 3}{\sqrt{12 \times 3}}$

Next work out **powers** or **roots**:    $\frac{6.25}{10} + \frac{19.1 \times 3}{6}$

Then **multiplication** and **division**:    $\frac{6.25}{10} + \frac{57.3}{6}$

Finally **addition** and **subtraction**:    $0.625 + 9.55 = 10.175$

You have to multiply the numbers under the $\sqrt{\ }$ before taking the square root.

You can **estimate** the answer to a calculation by rounding to 1 or 2 sf.

**example**

Estimate the answer to $\frac{3.7 \times 53.2}{18.94}$.

Round all numbers to 1 significant figure and then work out the calculation:
$\frac{4 \times 50}{20} = \frac{200}{20} = 10$, so 10 is an estimate for $\frac{3.7 \times 53.2}{18.94}$.

# Exercise N6

**1** Calculate: **a** $12 + \frac{14.7}{0.3}$ **b** $57 - \sqrt{9 \times 8 \times 18}$

**2** Work out: $3.22 + 0.003\,22$.

**3** Copy and complete:
$34 \div 10 = 34 \times 0.1$
$34 \div 10\,000 = 34 \times \ldots$

**4** Copy, complete and solve:

**a** $87.58 \div 0.4 = 875.8 \div \ldots = \ldots$
**b** $7.621 \div 0.05 = \ldots \div 5 = \ldots$
**c** $2.8 \div 0.008 = \ldots \div 8 = \ldots$

**5** Explain why the answer to $1 \div (\frac{1}{4} + \frac{1}{2})$ must be greater than 1.

Work out the answer. Give your answer as a fraction.

**6** Calculate: **a** $\frac{15.3}{\sqrt{9}} + \frac{2^3}{5-1}$ **b** $\frac{2}{5} + \frac{\sqrt{4^3 + 6^2}}{7.2 - 4.7}$

**7** Use these numbers to answer the following questions.
0.1    0.02    2.5    0.005    0.4    10    100    0.001

**a** Copy and complete: $0.02 \times \ldots = 2$
**b** Copy and complete: $2.5 \div \ldots = 2500$
**c** Copy and complete these sums.   $0.4 \times \ldots = 0.002$
$0.02 \times \ldots = 0.002$
**d** Choose two cards to give the lowest possible answer to:
  **i** $\ldots \times \ldots = \ldots$     **ii** $\ldots \div \ldots = \ldots$
**e** Choose two cards to give the highest possible answer to: $\ldots + \ldots = \ldots$
**f** Choose three different cards that multiply together to give an answer $\frac{1}{1000}$.

**8** Choose your answers from this list:
3    4    5    6    7

**a** Which is the best estimate to $8.3 \times 0.47$?
**b** Which is the best estimate to $73.2 \div 12.4$?

**9** Estimate the answer to: **a** $\frac{5.8 \times 19.2}{24.1}$ **b** $\frac{74.1 + 16.3}{19.4 - 4.9}$

**10** Show that $2 \times 10^5$ is 40 times bigger than $5 \times 10^3$.

**11** Choose your answers from this list:
0.00002    0.0002    0.002    0.02    0.2    2    20

**a** Which is the best estimate for $48.7 \times 0.0004$?
**b** Which is the best estimate for $48.7 \div 2.3$?

**12** Work out: $\frac{8.5^2 - 7.5^2}{\sqrt{8.5^2 - 7.5^2}}$.

**13** Work out: $2.9 + \sqrt{\dfrac{159 - (5 \times 1.8)}{7.5 \div 1.5}}$

**14** Explain how you know that $8.9 \times 10^6$ is smaller than $1.2 \times 10^7$ without writing out the numbers.

**15** A company wants to promote 200 g chocolate bars with a special offer.
These chocolate bars normally cost 92 pence.
The company could choose to:
  **i** increase the amount of chocolate in the bar by 25% or
  **ii** reduce the price of the bar by 25%.
Which should they choose to give the customer the better deal?
Show working to explain your answer.

**L6**

1 Look at these number cards:

a Choose a card to give the **lowest** possible answer to the calculation:

 =

b Now choose a card to give the **highest** possible answer.

2 a In a magazine there are three adverts on the same page.
Advert 1 uses $\frac{1}{4}$ of the page.
Advert 2 uses $\frac{1}{8}$ of the page.
Advert 3 uses $\frac{1}{16}$ of the page.
In **total**, what **fraction** of the page do the three adverts use?
Show your working.

b The cost of an advert is **£10** for each $\frac{1}{32}$ of a page.
An advert uses $\frac{3}{16}$ of a page. How much does the advert cost?

3 $\frac{1}{3}, \frac{1}{8}, \frac{1}{5}$ are all examples of unit fractions.
They all have a numerator that is 1, and a denominator that is greater than 1.
The ancient Egyptians used only unit fractions.
For $\frac{3}{4}$, they wrote the sum $\frac{1}{2} + \frac{1}{4}$.

a For what fraction did they write the sum $\frac{1}{2} + \frac{1}{5}$?
Show your working.

b They wrote $\frac{9}{20}$ as the sum of two unit fractions.
One of them was $\frac{1}{4}$.
What was the other?
Show your working.

**L7**

4 At an athletics meeting, the discus throws are measured to the nearest centimetre.

a Viv's best throw was measured as 35.42 m.
Could Viv's throw actually have been more than 35.42 m?
Explain your answer.

b Chris won the hurdles race in a time of 14.6 seconds measured to the nearest tenth of a second.
Between what two values does Chris's time actually lie?

5 a From the list, write the **best** estimate of the answer to
$72.34 \div 8.91$
6   7   8   9   10   11

b From the list, circle the **best** estimate of the answer to
$32.7 \times 0.48$
1.2   1.6   12   16   120   160

c Estimate the answer to $\dfrac{8.62 + 22.1}{5.23}$

Give your answer to **1 significant figure**.

d **Estimate** the answer to $\dfrac{28.6 \times 24.4}{5.67 \times 4.02}$

6 a Write the values of $k$ and $m$.
$64 = 8^2 = 4^k = 2^m$

b Copy and complete the following:
$2^{15} = 32\,768$
$2^{14} = \boxed{\phantom{00}}$

**L7**    **7**  Look at these number cards.

0.2  2  10  0.1  0.05  1

N3

**a** Choose two of the cards to give the **lowest possible answer** to the calculation:

$\square \times \square = \square$

**b** Choose two of the cards to give the answer **100**.

$\square \div \square = 100$

**8** The table shows some information about pupils in a school.

N4

|       | left-handed | right-handed |
|-------|-------------|--------------|
| girls | 32          | 180          |
| boys  | 28          | 168          |

There are **408 pupils** in the school.
**a** What **percentage** of the pupils are **boys**?
Show your working.
**b** What is the **ratio** of **left-handed** pupils to **right-handed** pupils?
Write your ratio in the form 1: ..........
Show your working.
**c** One pupil is chosen at random from the whole school.
What is the **probability** that the pupil chosen is a **girl** who is **right-handed**?

**L8**    **9**

N1

> Speed of light is about $1.1 \times 10^9$ km per hour
> Speed of sound is about $1.2 \times 10^3$ km per hour

**a** Calculate the speed of light in km per second.
Give your answer in standard form.
Show your working.
**b** How many times as fast as the speed of sound is the speed of light?
Give your answer to an appropriate degree of accuracy.
Show your working.
**c** Gary sees a flash of lightning.
25 second later he hears the sound of thunder.
Calculate how far away he is from the lightning.
(You do **not** need to include the speed of light in your calculation).
Show your working.

**10** For each of these cards **n** can be any positive number.

N2

$n^2$  $0.8n$  $\sqrt{n}$  $\frac{n}{0.8}$  $\frac{1}{n}$

The **answers** given by the cards are all positive numbers.
**a** Which card will **always** give an answer **less than n**?
**b** When **n is 1**, which cards will give the answer **1**?
**c** When **n is 4**, which cards will give an answer less than **4**?
**d** When **n is less than 1**, which cards will give an answer **less than n**?

A calculator uses the standard order of operations.
You need to watch out for hidden operations.

**KEYWORDS**
Power                    Rounding
Reciprocal               Standard form

▶ There is a hidden bracket in the denominator of a fraction.

> **example**
>
> Work out: $\frac{2.78 \times 6.9}{2.5 + 15.9}$
>
> You can use the memory for the denominator:
>
> [2] [.] [5] [+] [1] [5] [.] [9] [=] [M in] [AC]
>
> [2] [.] [7] [8] [×] [6] [.] [9] [÷] [MR] [=]
>
> or use brackets:
>
> [2] [.] [7] [8] [×] [6] [.] [9] [÷] [(] [2] [.] [5] [+] [1] [5] [.] [9] [)] [=]
>
> The answer is 1.0425.

▶ Press [×] between adjacent brackets.

> **example**
>
> Work out: $(37 - 6.25)(13.4 + 1.6)$
>
> Input: [(] [3] [7] [8] [−] [6] [.] [2] [5] [)] [×] [(] [1] [3] [.] [4] [+] [1] [.] [6] [)] [=]
>
> Display: 461.25

There are some special buttons that will make calculating simpler.

▷ You can use $\boxed{x^y}$ to find powers.

▷ The reciprocal button is $\boxed{\frac{1}{x}}$ or $\boxed{x^{-1}}$.

▷ Squaring and cubing have their own buttons, $\boxed{x^2}$ and $\boxed{x^3}$.

▷ You can input fractions and mixed numbers using $\boxed{a^{b/c}}$.

▷ You can change the sign of a number by using the $\boxed{(-)}$ or $\boxed{+/-}$ button.

▷ To input a number in standard form you can use the $\boxed{Exp}$ or $\boxed{EE}$ button.

▷ A calculator often displays the number 820 000 000 000 in standard form as $8.2^{11}$ or 8.2E11.

> You may need to put numbers in brackets before you use these special buttons.

You must give sensible answers to problems.

> **example**
>
> **a** Work out £25.99 ÷ 7.
> **b** A shelf 2 m long is filled with files 42 cm wide.
>    How many files are there?
>
> **a** Input: 25.99 ÷ 7 =
>    Display: 3.712857143
>    The answer is £3.71 (money answers should be given to a whole number of pence).
> **b** Input: 200 ÷ 42 =
>    Display: 4.761904762
>    The answer is 4 files (round down to the nearest whole number of files).

# Exercise N7

**L6** 1 The sides of a rectangle are given as $x$ and $12 - x$.
The area of the rectangle is 23 to the nearest whole number.
Area of rectangle $= x(12 - x) = 23$
Use the table to find between which one-decimal-place numbers $x$ lies.

| $x$ | $12 - x$ | Area |
|-----|----------|------|
| 1   | 11       | 11   |
| 2   | 10       |      |

2 Steve wants to find a value of $x$ that makes $x^2$ equal to $7 - x$.
He constructs a table that looks like this:

| $x$ | $x^2$ | $7 - x$ | Difference |
|-----|-------|---------|------------|
| 2   | 4     | 5       | 1          |
| 3   | 9     | 4       | 5          |

A value of $x$ lies between 2 and 3.
Use the table to find between which two one-decimal-place values this value of $x$ lies.
A second value of $x$ lies between $^-3$ and $^-4$.
Draw a new table and use it to find between which two one-decimal-places this value of $x$ lies.

**L7** 3 A car was driven at an average speed of 32 miles per hour.
The car used petrol at a rate of one litre for 13 km.

a Calculate how many litres of petrol were used in one hour of travel.
Show your working and write down the full calculator display. (5 miles = 8 km)
b Write your answer to a sensible degree of accuracy.

4 When a baby giraffe was born it was 1.36 m high.
It grew at a rate of an inch every 2 hours
Suppose it continued to grow at this rate.
About how many days old would the giraffe be when it was 4 m high?  Take 1 inch = 2.54 cm.

**L8** 5 $Q = r^3 + \frac{s - t^2}{s + t} - \frac{1}{r}$
Use the formula to work out the value of $Q$ when:

a $r = 50$      $s = 40$      $t = 30$
b $r = 21$      $s = 36$      $t = 25$
c $r = 1.25$     $s = 0.4$     $t = 0.6$
In each part:
i write down the full calculator display
ii write your answer to a sensible degree of accuracy.

6 The diameter of the Sun is $8.65 \times 10^5$ miles.
The diameter of the Earth is $7.92 \times 10^3$ miles.
How many times bigger is the diameter of the Sun than the diameter of the Earth?
Give your answer to a sensible degree of accuracy.

7 The formula for calculating the volume of a shape is: $V = h(a^2 - b^2)$.
Gemma substitutes the numbers $h = 4.3$, $a = 3.2$ and $b = 3.9$ into the formula.
Explain why her answer is not sensible.

8 The speed of light is approximately $7 \times 10^8$ miles per hour.
The speed of sound is approximately $7.5 \times 10^2$ miles per hour.
a Calculate in miles per second i the speed of light ii the speed of sound.
Give your answer in standard form.
b How many times faster than the speed of sound is the speed of light?
Give your answer to a sensible degree of accuracy.

An **expression** is a collection of numbers and letters linked by operations, but not including an equals sign.
Each part of an expression is called a **term**. Like terms have the same combination of letters.

You may need to expand brackets to simplify expressions.

▷ When multiplying out brackets, multiply all the terms inside the bracket by the term outside the bracket.
▷ When multiplying two brackets multiply each term in the first bracket with each term in the second bracket.

The sign in front of the term belongs to that term.

> **example**
>
> Expand:   **a** $3(2a - 5)$     **b** $5(a + 3) - 2(a - 4)$
>           **c** $(a + 3)(a + 2)$     **d** $(a + 7)(a - 4)$
> ........................................................................
> **a**  $6a - 15$
> **b**  $5a + 15 - 2a + 8 = 3a + 23$
> **c**  $a^2 + 2a + 3a + 6 = a^2 + 5a + 6$
> **d**  $a^2 - 4a + 7a - 28 = a^2 + 3a - 28$

Remember to collect like terms.

▶ When factorising, look for a number or letter that is common to each term.
▶ An expression that is the difference of two squares can factorise into two brackets:
$x^2 - y^2 = (x + y)(x - y)$

$3ab$ means $3 \times a \times b$.
$a^3$ means $a \times a \times a$.

> **example**
>
> Factorise:   **a** $3a - 15$   **b** $2a + ab$   **c** $a^2 - 9$   **d** $4a^2 - 25b^2$
> ........................................................................
> **a**  Common factor of 3: $3(a - 5)$
> **b**  Common factor of $a$: $a(2 + b)$
> **c**  Difference of two squares: $a^2 - 3^2 = (a + 3)(a - 3)$
> **d**  Difference of two squares: $(2a)^2 - (5b)^2 = (2a + 5b)(2a - 5b)$

You can use a power or index to simplify expressions.
You can only cancel terms that are multiplied so you may need to factorise first.

> **example**
>
> Simplify:   **a** $4a \times 3a^2$   **b** $a^4 \times a^3$   **c** $\frac{a^7}{a^2}$   **d** $\frac{a^3 b^2}{ab^2}$   **e** $\frac{a^5 b^3 + a^2 b}{a^4 b}$
> ........................................................................
> **a**  $4 \times 3 \times a^{1+2} = 12a^3$       **b**  $a^{4+3} = a^7$
> **c**  $a^{7-2} = a^5$                            **d**  $a^{3-1} b^{2-2} = a^2$
> **e**  Factorise the numerator and then cancel: $\frac{a^2 b(a^3 b^2 + 1)}{a^4 b} = \frac{a^3 b^2 + 1}{a^2}$

You can add or subtract algebraic fractions in the same way as you add and subtract ordinary fractions.

> **example**
>
> Explain if this statement is true or false. $\frac{1}{a} + \frac{1}{b} = \frac{2}{a + b}$
> ........................................................................
> $\frac{1}{a} + \frac{1}{b} = \frac{b}{ab} + \frac{a}{ab} = \frac{a + b}{ab}$, so the statement is false.

See N3 for adding fractions.

## Exercise A1

 **L6**

**1** Write each expression in its simplest form.

    **a** $(3a - 2) + (4a - 7)$     **b** $(2b + 5) - (b - 6)$     **c** $4c - (^-3c)$

**2** A rectangle has sides $n$ cm and 16 cm.

    **a** Write an expression for the perimeter of the rectangle.

The rectangle is cut in half lengthways and the halves placed side by side.

    **b** What is the perimeter of the new rectangle?
       Write the expression as simply as possible.

**3** This is a square tile.
The edge of the tile is $n$ cm long.
The perimeter of the tile is $4n$ cm.
The F-shape is made with 6 square tiles.
Write an expression for the perimeter of
the F-shape.

 **L7**

**4** Multiply out and simplify these expressions.
    **a** $4(2x + 3) - 2(3x + 4)$     **b** $5(x + 2) - 4(3 - 2x)$     **c** $3(3x - 2) - 4(5 - 2x)$

**5** Simplify $\frac{1}{a} - \frac{1}{b}$.

**6** In these walls, each brick is made by adding the two bricks underneath it.
Fill in the missing expressions in these walls.
Write your expression as simply as possible.

    **a**                          **b**

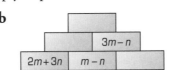

**7** Simplify these expressions, writing your answers as simply as possible.
    **a** $3ab \times 2b^3$     **b** $\frac{15a^3 b^2}{3abc}$

**8** Factorise these expressions as fully as possible.
    **a** $3x - 6$     **b** $6x^2 + 18x$

**9** Simplify:
    **a** $a^5 \times a^2$     **b** $ab^2 \times a^2$     **c** $4a^3 b^5 \times 3a$     **d** $a^{11} \div a^2$     **e** $6a^7 \div 2a^3$.

 **L8**

**10** Explain how you know that $(x + 5)^2$ is not equal to $x^2 + 25$.

**11** Multiply out and simplify these expressions.
    **a** $(x + 3)(x + 5)$     **b** $(x + 4)(x - 3)$     **c** $(x + 4)^2$     **d** $(x - 3)^2$

**12** Simplify $\dfrac{x^2 - y^2}{x + y}$.

**13** Simplify $\dfrac{x^5 y^2 + x^2 y^3}{4x^2 y}$.

**14** Multiply out and simplify these expressions.
    **a** $(x + 5)(x + 7)$     **b** $(x - 2)(x + 6)$     **c** $(x - 1)(x - 3)$

**15** Show that $(x + 3)^2 - (x + 2)^2$ simplifies to $2x + 5$.

You can find a value for an expression by substituting numbers for letters.

> **example**
>
> Evaluate: **a** $2x - 3y^2$ **b** $29 - (x + 2y) - y^3$ when $x = 7$ and $y = 2$.
>
> Replace $x$ with 7 and $y$ with 2:
> **a** $2 \times 7 - 3 \times 2^2 = 14 - 12 = 2$
> **b** $29 - (7 + 2 \times 2) - 2^3 = 29 - 11 - 8 = 10$

▷ Work out brackets first.
▷ Next work out powers or roots.
▷ Then multiply or divide.
▷ Finally add or subtract.

► An equation links two expressions with an equals sign.
  ▷ To solve an equation you do the same to both sides of the equals sign.
  ▷ Collect all terms with the letter on one side and all other terms on the other side.

> **example**
>
> Solve:   **a** $3x + 7 = 25$   **b** $7x - 3 = 5x + 11$
>
> **a** Subtract 7 from each side:   $3x = 18$
>    Divide both sides by 3:        $x = 6$
>
> **b** Subtract $5x$:          $2x - 3 = 11$
>    Add 3:               $2x = 14$
>    Divide by 2:          $x = 7$

► A **formula** is a statement that relates two or more letters.

Changing the subject of a formula means rearranging it so that a different letter is on its own (the subject).

> **example**
>
> Rearrange this equation to make $F$ the subject.     $C = \frac{5}{9}(F - 32)$
>
> Multiply by 9:        $9C = 5(F - 32)$
> Divide by 5:          $\frac{9C}{5} = F - 32$
> Add 32:               $\frac{9C}{5} + 32 = F$

A formula can show the relationship between two variables, for example the volume $V$, of a cube and the length, $a$, of its sides.

$V = a^3$

> **example**
>
> **a** Write a formula for the volume, $V$ of this prism.
> **b** Rearrange the formula to make $a$ the subject.
>
>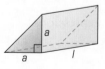
>
> The volume of a prism = area of cross-section × length.
>
> **a** Volume = area of triangle
>       × length
>    $V = \frac{1}{2} a \times a \times l$
>    $= \frac{1}{2}a^2 l$
>
> **b** Volume:              $V = \frac{1}{2}a^2 l$
>    Multiply by 2:        $2V = a^2 l$
>    Divide by $l$:        $\frac{2V}{l} = a^2$
>    Square root:        $\sqrt{\frac{2V}{l}} = a$

# Exercise A2

 **L6**

**1** You can use this formula to work out the cost of hiring a car.

$c = 27 + 2d$

$c$ is the cost in pounds and $d$ is the number of miles travelled.

  **a** A hire car is driven for 68 miles.
    What is the total cost of hiring the car?
  **b** The total cost of hiring a car is £209.
    Work out the number of miles the car travelled.

**2** Find $x$ and $y$.    **a** $\frac{3}{5} = \frac{x}{20}$    **b** $\frac{2}{5} = \frac{7}{y}$

**L7**

**3** When $x = 4.6$ and $y = 2.4$, work out the value of $(x + y)(x - y)$.

**4** Rearrange this equation to make $x$ the subject.

$y = 2(x + 7)$

**5** Rearrange the equation $y = 3(2a - x)$ to make $x$ the subject. Show your working.

**6** $y = \pm \sqrt{\frac{x^2 + 1}{x}}$

  **a** When $x = 4$ calculate the positive value of $y$.
    Show all the numbers on your calculator display.
  **b** When $x = 4$ give both values of $y$ correct to 3 significant figures.

**7** Solve these equations. Show your working.

  **a** $4x - 3 = x + 12$    **b** $2x - 7 = 13 - 3x$

**8** Solve these equation. Show your working.

  **a** $4x + 5 = 2x + 1$    **b** $2(x + 3) = 22$

**L8**

**9** Find the values of $x$ and $y$ when $p = 4$.

  **a** $x = \frac{3p^2}{2p - 3}$    **b** $y = \frac{(p - 2)(p + 3)}{7p}$

**10** For each of these cards, $n$ can be any positive number.
The answer given by the cards are all positive numbers.
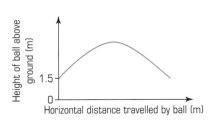
  **a** When $n$ is 1 which cards will give answer 1?
  **b** When $n$ is less than 1 which cards will give answer
    less than $n$?
  **c** When $n = 2$ which cards will give an answer greater than 2?
  **d** Which card will always give an answer greater than $n$?

 **11** Martha throws a ball to Kelly who is standing 30 m away.
The ball is thrown and caught at a height of 1.5 m above
the ground.
The ball follows the curve with equation $y = 4.5 + k(15 - x)^2$
where $k$ is a constant.
Calculate the value of $k$ by substituting $y = 1.5$, $x = 0$ into
the equation. Show your working.

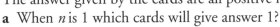

**12** These two rectangles have the same area.

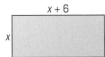

Use an algebraic method to find the value of $x$. Show your working.

You often need to form equations to solve problems.

KEYWORDS
Prove
Expression
Equation

**example**

This rectangle has perimeter of 24 cm.
Find $x$.

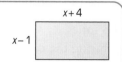

$P = 2(x - 1 + x + 4) = 4x + 6$
The perimeter is 24 cm, so $4x + 6 = 24$.
This gives $x = 4.5$ cm.

**example**

In the diagram, sides PQ and QR are equal.
The perimeter of the triangle is 95 cm.
Find the lengths of the sides.

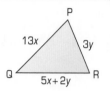

PQ and QR are equal so: $13x = 5x + 2y$
This gives $y = 4x$
The perimeter is $\qquad 13x + 5x + 2y + 3y = 95$
$\qquad\qquad\qquad\qquad\quad 18x + 5y = 95$
Substitute $y = 4x$: $\qquad\quad 18x + 20x = 95$
$\qquad\qquad\qquad\qquad\qquad 38x = 95$
$\qquad\qquad\qquad\qquad x = 2.5$ cm and $y = 10$ cm
Therefore PQ = 32.5 cm, QR = 32.5 and PR = 30 cm.

▶ You can prove that a statement is true by giving a chain of reasons.
▶ You can show that a statement is false by giving an example that doesn't work.

**example**

$x^3$ represents a cubed number, where $x$ is an integer.

**a** Explain how you know there are values for $x$ for which $8 + x^3$ does not represent a cubed number.
**b** Explain why the expression $8x^3$ must represent a cubed number.

**a** For example, when $x = 1$, $8 + x^3 = 9$, which is not a cube number.
**b** 8 is a cube number ($2^3 = 8$). Two cube numbers multiplied together will always give another cube number. Or using algebra: $8x^3 = (2x)^3$.

**example**

Which of these statements is true?

**i** When $x$ is even $(x + 1)^2$ is odd.
**ii** When $x$ is odd $(x + 1)^2$ is odd.

Statement **i** is true.
$(x + 1)^2$ represents a square number.
If $x$ is even and you add 1 then you get an odd number.
An odd number squared is an odd number.

## Exercise A3

L6

**1** I think of a number. Multiplying my number by six and adding one is the same as multiplying my number by two and adding seven.
I called my number $x$ and formed an equation: $6x + 1 = 2x + 7$.
Solve this equation and write down the value of $x$. Show your working.

**2** I think of a number. Doubling my number and adding five is the same as multiplying my number by four and taking away two.
Form an equation and solve it to find the number I was thinking of.

**3** David had 5 bags of marbles and John had 3 bags of marbles. Each bag contained the same number of marbles, $m$. David was given 1 marble and John was given 9 marbles.
The number of marbles they each had was now the same.
Find how many marbles there were in each bag.

**M**

**4 a** Two numbers multiply together to make ⁻18.
They add together to make 7.
What are the two numbers?
**b** Two numbers multiply together to make ⁻18.
They add together to make ⁻7.
What are the two numbers?
**c** Two numbers multiply together to make 24.
They add together to make ⁻11.
What are the two numbers?

L7

**5** Which of the following statements is true? Explain your reasons.
A  When $x$ is even $(x + 2)(x + 1)$ is even.    B  When $x$ is odd $(x + 2)(x + 1)$ is odd.

**6** If $x$ is an integer, explain how you know that the expression $25x^2$ must represent a square number.

**7** Copy this table. Tick the correct box for each algebraic statement.

| Correct for: | no values of $x$ | one value of $x$ | two values of $x$ | all values of $x$ |
|---|---|---|---|---|
| $2x - 5 = 17$ | | | | |
| $4(x + 2) = 4x + 8$ | | | | |
| $x - 1 = x + 1$ | | | | |
| $x - 7 = 7 - x$ | | | | |
| $x^2 = 16$ | | | | |

L8

**8** These two rectangles have the same area.
Use an algebraic method to find the value of $x$.

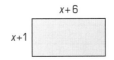
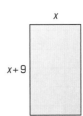

**9** The perimeter of this triangle is 31 cm.
Sides PQ and QR are the same length.
Find the values of $x$ and $y$.
(All lengths are given in cm.)

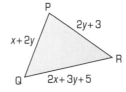

**10** $x^2$ represents a square number; $x$ is an integer.
**a** Think about the expression $49 + x^2$.
Explain how you know that there are values of $x$ for which $49 + x^2$ does not represent a square number.
**b** Explain why the expression $49x^2$ must represent a square number.

23

**Trial and improvement**

When an equation is complicated you can find an approximate solution using trial and improvement.

**example**

$y = x^2 - 5x + 3$
There is a value of $x$ between 0 and 1 that makes $y = 0$.
There is also a value of $x$ between 4 and 5 that makes $y = 0$.
Find these values of $x$ to 1 dp.

| | | | | | | |
|---|---|---|---|---|---|---|
| Try $x = 0.5$ | $y = 0.75$ | too high | Try $x = 4.2$ | $y = \,^-0.36$ | too low |
| Try $x = 0.6$ | $y = 0.36$ | too high | Try $x = 4.3$ | $y = \,^-0.01$ | too low |
| Try $x = 0.7$ | $y = \,^-0.01$ | too low | Try $x = 4.4$ | $y = 0.36$ | too high |
| Try $x = 0.65$ | $y = 0.1725$ | too high | Try $x = 4.35$ | $y = 0.1725$ | too high |

$x$ is between 0.65 and 0.7     $x$ is between 4.3 and 4.35
so $x = 0.7$ to 1 dp.        so $x = 4.3$ to 1 dp.

Once you know $x$ is between 0.6 and 0.7, substitute the halfway value to see which is the best estimate.

Approximate solutions can also be found from a graph.

You can read off the solutions at $y = 0$ (where the graph cuts the $x$-axis).

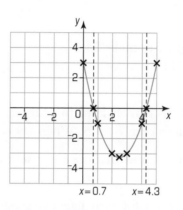

$x = 0.7$     $x = 4.3$

See A6 for graph drawing.

The roots are the values of $x$ that make an equation correct.

**example**

Find the roots of the equation $2x^2 = 3x + 1$.

Work out the value of $2x^2$ and $3x + 1$ and find the difference between them.

| $x$ | $2x^2$ | $3x + 1$ | $2x^2 - (3x - 1)$ | |
|---|---|---|---|---|
| $^-2$ | 8 | $^-5$ | 13 | too high |
| $^-1$ | 2 | $^-2$ | 4 | too high |
| 0 | 0 | 1 | $^-1$ | too low |
| 1 | 2 | 4 | $^-2$ | too low |
| 2 | 8 | 7 | 1 | too high |

One root lies between $^-1$ and 0.
Another root lies between 1 and 2.

Roots lie between values where the difference changes from too high to too low.
You can try values of $x$ to 1 dp to find more accurate roots.

## Exercise A4

**L6** **1** Some students started to solve this equation in different ways: $7x - 2 = 3x + 10$.

**a** Which is correct?

A
| | |
|---|---|
| $7x - 2 = 3x + 10$ |
| so $5x = 13x$ |

B
| |
|---|
| $7x - 2 = 3x + 10$ |
| so $10x = 8$ |

C
| |
|---|
| $7x - 2 = 3x + 10$ |
| so $4x = 12$ |

**b** A different pupil used trial and improvement to solve the equation.
Explain why trial and improvement is not a good method to use.

**L7** **2** The table below shows values of $x$ and $y$ for the equation $y = x^2 + x - 1$.
**a** Copy and complete the table.

| $x$ | $^-3$ | $^-2$ | $^-1$ | 0 | 1 | 2 | 3 |
|---|---|---|---|---|---|---|---|
| $y$ | 5 | 1 | $^-1$ | $^-1$ | 1 | | |

The value of $y$ is 0 for values of $x$ between 0 and 1 and between $^-2$ and $^-1$.
**b** Use trial and improvement to find the values of $x$, to one decimal place, that give the value of $y$ closest to 0.

| $x$ | $y$ |
|---|---|
| 0 | $^-1$ |
| 1 | 1 |

| $x$ | $y$ |
|---|---|
| $^-2$ | 1 |
| $^-1$ | $^-1$ |

**3** James wants to find a value for $x$ such that $x^3 = 5 + x$.
The table shows that the value of $x$ lies between 1 and 2.

| $x$ | $x^3$ | $5 + x$ |
|---|---|---|
| 1 | 1 | 6 |
| 2 | 8 | 7 |

Use trial and improvement to find the value of $x$ correct to one decimal place.

**4** The stopping distance of a car can be estimated using the formula $D = \frac{S^2 + 3S}{25}$
where $S$ is the speed of the car in km/h and $D$ is the stopping distance in m.
**a** After an accident skid marks 50 m long were measured on the road.
The table shows the car was travelling at a speed between 30 and 40 km/h.

| $S$ | 20 | 30 | 40 |
|---|---|---|---|
| $D = \frac{S^2 + 3S}{25}$ | 18.4 | 39.6 | 68.8 |

Find an estimate for the speed of the car correct to the nearest 1 km/h
**b** In a second accident skid marks 80 m long were measured on the road.
Find an estimate for the speed of the car correct to the nearest 1 km/h for this accident.

**L8** **5** The equation $3x^2 = 5x + 1$ has one positive root between the values $x = 1$ and $x = 2$.
**a** Try some values of $x$ to one decimal place to find between which two numbers, given to one decimal place, the root lies.
Use a copy of the table below to show your trials.

| $x$ | $3x^2$ | $5x + 1$ | Difference |
|---|---|---|---|
| | | | |
| | | | |
| | | | |

**b** Try some 2 decimal place numbers for $x$.
Between which two numbers, given to two decimal places, does the root for $x$ lie?

**6** Find all integer values for $n$ that satisfy both these inequalities:
$\frac{1}{2}n(n + 1) > 270$ and $\frac{1}{2}n(n + 1) < 320$
You may use trial and improvement.

▶ A sequence is a set of numbers, objects or terms that follow a rule.
▶ A linear or arithmetic sequence increases by the same amount each time.

You can generate terms of a sequence using either:

▶ a term-to-term rule or
▶ a position-to-term rule.

**example**

a Find the next 2 terms of this sequence: 3, 6, 12, 24, ...
b Find the first 4 terms of a sequence described by $4n - 1$.

a The terms are doubling each time, next 2 terms are 48 and 96.
b Substitute $n = 1, 2, 3, 4$ to generate terms 3, 7, 10, 13.

You can use differences to find the $n$th term of a sequence.

**example**

Find the $n$th term of these sequences.

a 5, 7, 9, 11, ... b 2, 5, 10, 17, 26, ...

a First differences: 2, 2, 2, ...
So the rule has $2n$ term.
Adjusting for the first term,
$n$th term is $2n + 3$.

b First differences: 3, 5, 7, 9, ...
Second differences: 2, 2, 2, ...
So the rule has $n^2$ term.
Adjusting for the first term, $n$th term is $n^2 + 1$.

A linear sequence will have a constant first difference.
A linear sequence will have highest power $n^1$.

A quadratic sequence will have a constant second difference.
A quadratic sequence will have highest power $n^2$.

You can use sequences in practical situations.

**example**

Find the 50th triangular number.

The triangle numbers are 1, 3, 6, 10, 15, 21, ...
First differences: 2, 3, 4, 5, 6, ...
Second differences: 1, 1, 1, 1, ...
So rule has $n^2$ term.
Adjusting for the first term, $n$th term $T(n) = \frac{1}{2}n^2 + \frac{1}{2}n$.
(Check it works for second and third terms.)
To find the 50th triangle number, substitute $n = 50$ into the formula for the $n$th term.

$T = \frac{1}{2}(50)^2 + \frac{1}{2} \times 50$
$= 1275.$

When you adjust for the first term if the sequence is linear you can add or subtract a number, if the sequence is quadratic you can add or subtract a term in $n$ and/or a number.

## Exercise A5

**L6**

**1** A pattern is made from blue and white tiles.

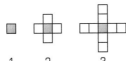

Pattern     1     2     3

**a** How many blue tiles and how many white tiles will there be in these patterns?
  **i** pattern 6    **ii** pattern 10    **iii** pattern P

**b** $T$ = total number of blue and white tiles, $P$ = pattern number.
Write an equation connecting $T$ and $P$.

**2** For each of the following sequences:
  **i** Write down the next two terms.
  **ii** Find a rule for the $n$th term.
  **a** 7, 11, 15, 19, ...
  **b** 7, 15, 23, 31, ...
  **c** 1, 4, 9, 16, ...
  **d** 2, 5, 10, 17, ...

**L7**

**3** Each term in this sequence is made by adding 1 to the numerator and 3 to the denominator:
$$\frac{1}{2}, \frac{2}{5}, \frac{3}{8}, \frac{4}{11}, \ldots$$
Write an expression for the $n$th term of the sequence.

**4** The $n$th term of a sequence is $\dfrac{2n-1}{2n+1}$.

The first term of the sequence is $\frac{1}{3}$.
Write down the next three terms of this sequence.

**5** Look at this part of a number line:
  **a** Fill in the two missing numbers.
  **b** Copy and complete this sentence.
    The numbers on this number line go up in steps of ...

    -3    __    1    3    5    7    __    11

**6** Sammy is using square patterns of dots to find expressions for $n^2$.

$$3^2 = 2^2 + 2 + 3 \qquad 4^2 = 3^2 + 3 + 4 \qquad 5^2 = 4^2 + 4 + 5$$

Sammy wants to write an expression for $n^2$ using her diagrams.
Write down an expression for $n^2$.

**L8**

**7** The table shows the number of buckets of water, of different capacities,
needed to fill a paddling pool of capacity 360 litres.

**a** Copy and complete the table.
**b** Write an equation to connect
$P$ (the capacity of the paddling
pool), $B$ (the capacity of a bucket) and $N$ (the number of buckets).

| Capacity of bucket (litres) | 2 | 5 | 6 | | | 12 |
|---|---|---|---|---|---|---|
| Number of buckets | | | 60 | 45 | 36 | |

**8** The table shows the number of days it takes to dig a hole depending on
the number of workmen that are digging.

**a** Copy and complete the table.
**b** Write an equation to connect
the hole size, $H$, the number of
men, $M$, and the number of days, $D$.

| Number of men | 1 | | 4 | 5 | | 10 |
|---|---|---|---|---|---|---|
| Number of days | | 30 | 15 | | | |

**L6**

**1** Write each expression in its simplest form.
  **i** $(3d + 5) + (d - 2)$
  **ii** $3m - (-m)$

**A2**

**L7**

**2** Bryn wants to use the formulae

$$P = s + t + \frac{5\sqrt{s^2 + t^2}}{3} \text{ and } A = \frac{1}{2}st + \frac{(s^2 + t^2)}{9}$$

to work out the perimeter ($P$) and area ($A$) of shapes like this:

**N7**

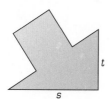

For this shape, Bryn substitutes $s = 4.5$ and $t = 6$ into the formulae.

**a** Work out the values of:
  **i** $4.5 + 6 + \frac{5 \times \sqrt{4.5^2 + 6^2}}{3}$.
  **ii** $\frac{1}{2} \times 4.5 \times 6 + \frac{(4.5^2 + 6^2)}{9}$.

For this shape, Bryn substitutes $s = 1.7$ and $t = 0.9$ into the formulae.

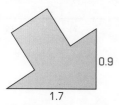

**b** Work out the values of:
  **i** $1.7 + 0.9 + \frac{5 \times \sqrt{1.7^2 + 0.9^2}}{3}$.
  **ii** $\frac{1}{2} \times 1.7 \times 0.9 + \frac{\sqrt{1.7^2 + 0.9^2}}{9}$.

**3** This is what a pupil wrote:

**A1**

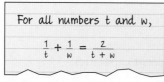

For all numbers $t$ and $w$,

$$\frac{1}{t} + \frac{1}{w} = \frac{2}{t + w}$$

Show that the pupil was **wrong**.

**4 a** The subject of the equation below is $p$.
    $$p = 2(e + f)$$
    Rearrange the equation to make $e$ the subject.
  **b** Rearrange the equation $r = \frac{1}{2}(c - d)$ to make $d$ the subject.
    Show your working.

**A1**

**L7**

**5 a** Find the values of $a$ and $b$ when $p = 10$.    **A2**

   **i** $a = \frac{3p^3}{2}$

   **ii** $b = \frac{2p^2(p-3)}{7p}$

**b** Simplify this expression as fully as possible.

   $\frac{3cd^2}{5cd}$

**c** Multiply out and simplify these expressions.

   **i** $3(x-2) - 2(4-3x)$

   **ii** $(x+2)(x+3)$

   **iii** $(x+4)(x-1)$

   **iv** $(x-2)^2$

**6** Equations may have different numbers of solutions.    **A3**
For example: $x + 2 = 7$ has only one solution, $x = 5$
but $x + 1 + 2 = x + 3$ is true for all values of $x$.
Copy the table and tick (✓) the correct box for each algebraic statement.

| | Correct for **no** values of $x$ | Correct for **one** value of $x$ | Correct for **two** values of $x$ | Correct for **all** values of $x$ |
|---|---|---|---|---|
| $3x + 7 = 8$ | | | | |
| $3(x + 1) = 3x + 3$ | | | | |
| $x + 3 = x - 3$ | | | | |
| $5 + x = 5 - x$ | | | | |
| $x^2 = 9$ | | | | |

**7 a** Pupils started to solve the equation $6x + 8 = 4x + 11$ in different ways.    **A4**
For each statement **i** to **vi**, write down whether it is true or false.

   **i**         $6x + 8 = 4x + 11$        **ii**         $6x + 8 = 4x + 11$
      so       $14x = 15x$                so    $6x + 4x = 11 + 8$

   **iii**       $6x + 8 = 4x + 11$        **iv**        $6x + 8 = 4x + 11$
      so        $6x = 4x + 3$               so      $2x + 8 = 11$

   **v**        $6x + 8 = 4x + 11$        **vi**        $6x + 8 = 4x + 11$
      so         $2x = 3$                 so       $^-3 = \,^-2x$

**b** A different pupil used trial and improvement to solve the equation $6x + 8 = 4x + 11$.
Explain why trial and improvement is not a good method to use.

**8** The table below shows values of $x$ and $y$ for the equation $y = x^2 + x - 5$.    **A4**
**a** Copy and complete the table.

| $x$ | $^-2$ | $^-1$ | $0$ | $1$ | $2$ | $3$ |
|---|---|---|---|---|---|---|
| $y$ | | | | $^-3$ | $1$ | $7$ |

The value of $y$ is 0 for a value of $x$ between 1 and 2.
**b** Find the value of $x$, to 1 decimal place, that gives the value of $y$ closest to 0.
You may use trial and improvement.

| $x$ | $y$ |
|---|---|
| $1$ | $^-3$ |
| $2$ | $1$ |

**L8**

**9 a** Explain how you know that $(y + 3)^2$ is not equal to $y^2 + 9$.    **A4**
**b** Multiply out and simplify these expressions.

   **i** $(y+2)(y+5)$

   **ii** $(y-6)(y-6)$

   **iii** $(3y-8)(2y+5)$

To draw a graph from its equation:

▶ Use the equation to work out values of $y$ for different values of $x$.
▶ Plot each $(x, y)$ and join the points.

Draw these lines.
**a** $y = x$  **b** $y = 2x$  **c** $y = 3x - 1$  **d** $x + y = 5$

Generate at least three points for each graph:

| $x$ | ⁻1 | 0 | 1 |
|---|---|---|---|
| **a** $y = x$ | ⁻1 | 0 | 1 |
| **b** $y = 2x$ | ⁻2 | 0 | 2 |
| **c** $y = 3x - 1$ | ⁻4 | ⁻1 | 2 |
| **d** $x + y = 5$ | 6 | 5 | 4 |

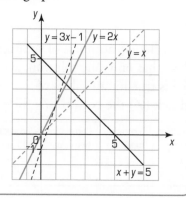

You should be able to draw horizontal lines like $y = 4$ and vertical lines like $x = 2$ without drawing a table of values.

▶ The general equation of a straight line is $y = mx + c$ where $m$ is the gradient of the line and $c$ is where the line crosses the $y$-axis (the $y$-intercept).
A line with gradient $m = 3$ and $y$-intercept $c = 2$ has equation $y = 3x + 2$.

Find the equations of these lines.

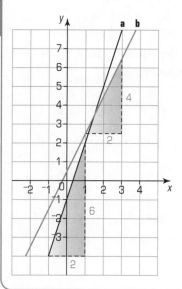

**a** The line crosses the $y$-axis at ⁻1, so $c = $ ⁻1.
The gradient $= 6 \div 2 = 3$, so $m = 3$.
The equation is $y = 3x - 1$.
**b** The line crosses the $y$-axis at $\frac{1}{2}$, so $c = \frac{1}{2}$.
The gradient $= 4 \div 2 = 2$, so $m = 2$.
The equation is $y = 2x + \frac{1}{2}$.

## Exercise A6

**L6**

1   Sketch the graphs of:

   **a** $y = x$     **b** $y = {}^-3$     **c** $x = 2$

2   Does the point $(20, 60)$ lie on the line $y = 3x$? Explain how you know.

3   Does the point $(2, 7)$ lie on the line $y = 2x + 1$? Explain how you know.

**L7**

4   Look at this graph.

   **a** The line through points A and B has equation $y = 0$.
      What is the equation of the line through C and E?
   **b** The line through the points A and E has equation $x + y = 1$.
      What is the equation of the line through B and D?

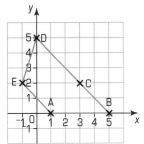

5   Draw the graphs of:

   **a** $x + y = 4$     **b** $y = 2x + 3$

6   Here are five equations. Think about the graphs of these equations.
   A: $y = 3x + 1$     B: $y = x^3$     C: $y = 3x - 2$     D: $x = 3$     E: $y = 3$

   **a** Which two graphs go through the point $(3, 3)$?
   **b** Which graph is parallel to the $x$-axis?
   **c** Which graph is not a straight line?
   **d** Which graphs have the same gradient?

**L8**

7   Look at the graph.
   The gradient of the straight line is 0.25

   **a** Show how you can work this out from the graph.
   **b** What is the equation of the straight line?
   **c** Write down an equation of a straight line that is
      parallel to the one shown.

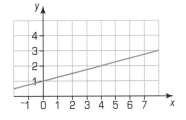

8   Look at this hexagon.

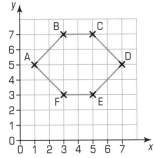

   **a** What is the equation of the line through these points?
      **i** B and F     **ii** E and F
   **b** Which two points does the line with equation $y + x = 6$ pass through?
   **c** This hexagon has two lines of symmetry.
      Copy the diagram and draw on these lines of symmetry.
      Write down the equations of the lines of symmetry.

9   Look at the graph.
   **a** The gradient of the line through A and B is $^-2$.
      Show how you can work this out from the graph.
   **b** What is the equation of the straight line through A
      and B?
   **c** Write down an equation of a straight line that is
      parallel to the line through A and B.

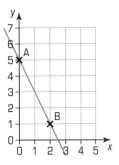

A quadratic function contains a squared term.
The graph of an equation with a squared term will be a curve.

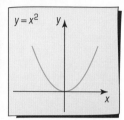 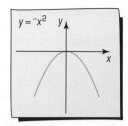

If $x^2$ is positive the curve will be U-shaped.
If the equation has a $^-x^2$ term the curve will be upside down.

If, in the equation, a number has been added or subtracted the curve moves up or down.

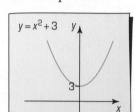 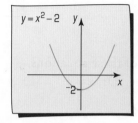 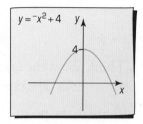

The mathematical name for these curves is 'parabola'.

If the $x^2$ term is multiplied by a number then the curve gets more squashed or more spread out.

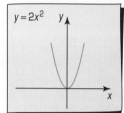 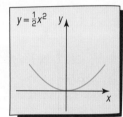

---

**example**

The graph shows the curve $y = x^2 - 9$.
What are the coordinates of the points where the curve crosses the $x$-axis?

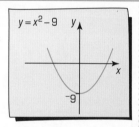

Points on the $x$-axis have $y = 0$.
So $x^2 - 9 = 0$, giving $x = 3$ or $^-3$.
The coordinates of the points are $(^-3, 0)$ and $(3, 0)$.

---

**example**

The curve $y = x^2 - 9$ is reflected in the line $x = 2$.
What are the coordinates of the points where the new curve crosses the $x$-axis?

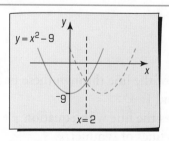

$(1, 0)$ and $(7, 0)$

---

**example**

The curve $y = x^2 - 9$ is reflected in the line $y = ^-4$
What is the equation of the new curve?

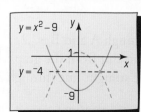

The graph is upside-down so $x^2$ is negative:
$y = ^-x^2 + 1$

# Exercise A7

**L8**

1 The graph shows the graph with equation $y = {}^-x^2$.

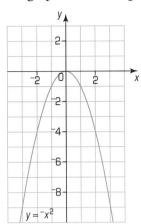

$y = {}^-x^2$

a Copy the graph. On the same axes sketch the graph with equation $y = {}^-2x^2$.

b Curve A is the reflection in the $x$-axis of $y = {}^-x^2$. What is the equation of curve A?

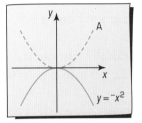

2 The diagram shows a sketch of the curve $y = x^2 - 4$.

a What are the coordinates of the points where the curve crosses:

  i the $x$-axis     ii the $y$-axis?

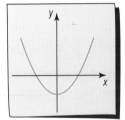

b The curve is translated one unit up on the $y$-axis What is the equation of the translated curve?

c The curve is reflected in the $x$-axis.

  i What are the coordinates of the point where the new curve crosses the $y$-axis?

  ii What is the equation of the new curve?

3 The diagram shows a sketch of the curve $y = 9 - x^2$.

a What are the coordinates of the points where the curve crosses:

  i the $x$-axis     ii the $y$-axis?

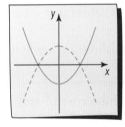

b The curve $y = 9 - x^2$ is reflected in the line $y = 5$. What is the equation of the new curve?

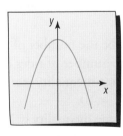

4 The diagram shows a sketch of the curve $y = x^2 - 3$. Choose from the list below the inequalities that fully describe the shaded region

$y \leqslant x^2 - 3$     $y \geqslant x^2 - 3$     $x \leqslant 0$     $x \geqslant 0$     $y \leqslant 0$     $y \geqslant 0$

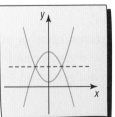

Simultaneous equations are two equations whose unknowns have the same value.

You can solve simultaneous equations by finding where their graphs meet or by an algebraic method.

**example**

Solve these simultaneous equations.
$x + y = 6$ and $y = 2x + 3$

.........................................................................................................

Draw the graphs of the equations:
The lines meet at $(1, 5)$.
So the solution is $x = 1$ and $y = 5$.

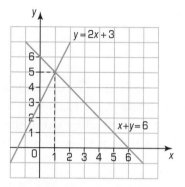

To solve algebraically you can use substitution.
Substitute $y = 2x + 3$ into $x + y = 6$, giving:
$$x + 2x + 3 = 6$$
$$3x + 3 = 6$$
$$3x = 3$$
$$x = 1$$
Substituting $x = 1$ into either of the original equations gives $y = 5$.

An inequality is a relationship between two terms that are comparable, but not equal.

   $<$ means 'less than'      $>$ means 'greater than'

An inequality has a range of values as its solution.
For example, the integer values that satisfy the inequality $x > 3$ are $x = 4, 5, 6, 7, \ldots$

You can represent inequalities on a graph to solve problems.

**example**

At a fair, dodgem rides cost £1 and Ferris wheel rides costs £2. I have £10 to spend.
A dodgem ride lasts for 15 minutes, whereas a Ferris wheel ride takes 5 minutes.
I have only 1 hour at the fair. How many rides can I go on?

.........................................................................................................

Let $d$ be the number of rides on the dodgems and $f$ be the number of rides on the Ferris wheel:
The cost inequality is $d + 2f \leqslant 10$, so draw the line $d + 2f = 10$.
The time inequality is $15d + 5f \leqslant 60$, or $3d + 5f \leqslant 12$ ($\div 5$), so draw the line $3d + f = 12$.

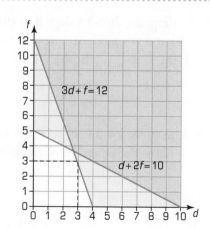

The greatest number of rides is 6:
3 on the dodgems and 3 on the Ferris wheel, or 2 on the dodgems and 4 of the Ferris wheel.

# Exercise A8

L6

**1 a** Two numbers multiply together to make 20 and add together to make 9.
What are the two numbers?

**b** Two numbers multiply together to make ⁻20 and add together to make 1.
What are the two numbers?

**L7**

**2 a** On the same graph draw the lines $y = 2x - 1$ and $y = x + 3$.
Use axes from 0 to 8.

**b** Solve the simultaneous equations $y = 2x - 1$ and $y = x + 3$.

**3** Solve these simultaneous equations to find the values of $x$ and $y$. Show your working.

**a** $y = 2x + 1, y = 4x - 2$　　**b** $x + 6y = 13, x + y = 4$　　**c** $y = 3x - 8, 7y = x + 7$

**4** One week Josh received £6.50 for delivering 50 newspapers and 200 flyers.
The next week Josh received £6.80 for delivering 40 newspapers and 240 flyers.

Call the amount received for each newspaper $x$ and the amount received for each flyer $y$. Use simultaneous equations to work out how much Josh would receive if he delivered 60 newspapers and 120 flyers. You may want to write the total amount received in pence. Show your working.

**M** **5** Write down the integer solutions of this inequality: $2 \leqslant x < 8$.

**6 a** 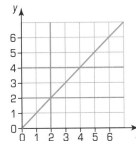 **b**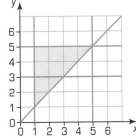

One region can be described by these inequalities:
$y \leqslant x, y \leqslant 4, y \geqslant 2, x > 2$
Put an R in the region described.

The shaded region can be described by three inequalities.
Write down these inequalities.

 **7** Find the smallest value for $n$ such that　　$n(n + 2) > 500$.

**8 a** On the same graph draw the lines $y = 2x - 5$, and $y = 1 - x$.
Use axes from ⁻2 to 4.

**b** Use your graph to solve these simultaneous equations:
$y = 2x - 5$
$y = 1 - x$.

**M** **9** Look at this inequality:　　$8.7 < n \leqslant 12$.
Write down all the integer solutions.

**M** **10** Look at this inequality:　　$⁻2 < n \leqslant 5.2$.
Write down all the integer solutions.

**L8**

**11** Solve these inequalities.

**a** $\dfrac{3(x - 2)}{2} \geqslant 6$　　**b** $\dfrac{2(4x + 1)}{5} \leqslant 6$

**12** Explain why $x^2 < 4$ does not mean that $x < 2$.

**13** Solve the simultaneous equations $3x + y = 5$ and $5x - y = 3$.
Show your working.

**14** Solve the simultaneous equations $2x + y = 5$ and $6x + y = 7$.
Show your working.

You can use algebra and graphs to solve problems involving proportion.

**example**

This graph shows the conversion of miles to kilometres.
Use the graph to convert:

**a**  6.2 miles to kilometres  **b**  7 km to miles

Reading from the graph:

**a**  9.9 km
**b**  4.4 miles

Using algebra is more accurate.
The equation of the graph is
$y = 1.6x$.

**a**  $6.2 \times 1.6 = 9.92$ km
**b**  $7 \div 1.6 = 4.375$ miles

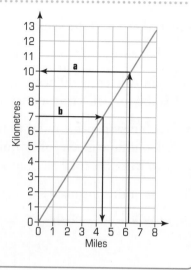

See N5 for ratio and proportion.

You may be asked to plot, interpret and discuss graphs.

Speed can be found from distance–time graphs.
You need to know the relationship between speed, distance and time.

$$\text{Speed} = \frac{\text{distance}}{\text{time}} \qquad \text{Time} = \frac{\text{distance}}{\text{speed}} \qquad \text{Distance} = \text{speed} \times \text{time}$$

**example**

It takes me 45 minutes to walk 3 miles home from school.
What is my average speed?

45 minutes = $\frac{3}{4}$ hour
Average speed = distance ÷ time = $3 \div \frac{3}{4} = 4$ mph (miles per hour)

**example**

This graph shows a cyclist's journey.

**a**  When does the cyclist stop for a rest?
    How can you tell?
**b**  How far away from home is the cyclist after 20 minutes?
**c**  What is the greatest speed?
**d**  Why does the graph slope downwards after 55 minutes?
**e**  What is the cyclist's average speed on the final section of the journey?

**a**  Between 20 and 30 minutes and 45 and 55 minutes.
    The graph is horizontal.
**b**  4 km
**c**  The steepest section gives the greatest speed:
    $6.5 \div \frac{1}{4} = 26$ km/h (15 minutes = $\frac{1}{4}$ hour)
**d**  The cyclist is returning home.
**e**  $10.5 \div \frac{35}{60} = 18$ km/h

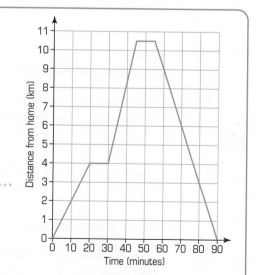

## Exercise A9

**L6**

**1** Mobile phone providers make different charges for calls.
The graph shows how much two different price plans charge each month for calls.

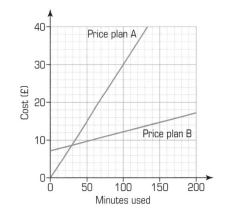

  **a** How much would you pay if you made 40 minutes of calls on price plan A?

  **b** If one month you were charged £13.00 on price plan B. How many minutes had you used the mobile phone in that month?

  **c** Copy and complete these sentences.

  **i** On price plan A you pay ... for each minute of calls.

  **ii** On price plan B you pay ... plus ... for each minute of calls.

  **d** When would it would be cheaper to be on price plan B instead of price plan A?

**L7** **M**

**2** A cheetah runs at a speed of 120 km per hour.
At this speed how far does it go in 2 minutes?

**3** The line shows the distance between home, school and town centre.
It also shows information about journey times.

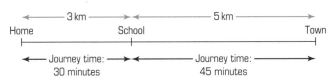

  **a** What is the average speed, in km per hour, of the journey from:
  **i** home to school   **ii** school to town?

  **b** One day I go to school and then straight into town.
  What is my average speed, in km per hour, for this journey?

**4** The graph shows the depth of water in a bath.
From A to B both taps are turned full on.

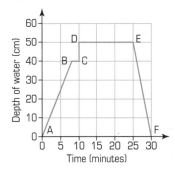

  **a** What time did someone get into the bath?
  **b** What might be happening from C to D?
  **c** How long did it take for the bath water to empty out?

**L8**

**5** Reuben winds up a toy car and lets it go.
The car accelerates in a straight line until it reaches its top speed.
It then hits a brick wall.

  **a** Which one of these graphs shows the journey of the toy car?

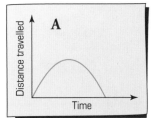
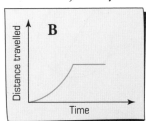
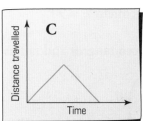

  **b** Explain why each of the other two graphs are wrong.

You should learn these angle facts:

▷ Angles on a straight line add to 180°.
▷ Angles around a point add to 360°.
▷ Angles in a triangle add to 180°.
▷ Angles in a quadrilateral add to 360°.
▷ Exterior angle of a triangle = sum of two interior opposite angles.

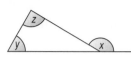

$x = y + z$

**KEYWORDS**
Quadrilateral       Corresponding
Alternate           Semicircle
Triangle            Tangent
Vertically opposite

**example**

Work out the angles marked with letters.

**a**

**b**

**c**

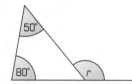

**a** $p + 20° + 20° = 180°$
(angles in a triangle)
So $p = 140°$

**b** $q + 90° + 60° + 100° = 360°$
(angles in a quadrilateral)
So $q = 110°$

**c** $r = 50° + 80°$
(exterior angle in a triangle)
So $r = 130°$

Angles are formed when lines cross. You should learn these three angle facts:

Vertically opposite angles
are equal.

$a = b$

Alternate angles
are equal.

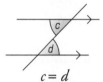

$c = d$

Corresponding angles
are equal.

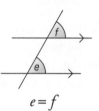

$e = f$

**example**

Work out the angles marked with letters.

**a**

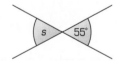

**b**

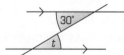

**c**

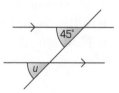

**a** $s = 55°$
(vertically opposite angles)

**b** $t = 30°$
(alternate angles)

**c** $u = 45°$
(corresponding angles)

You should know these two angle facts in circles.

▷ Angle in a semicircle is 90°.

▷ Angle between tangent and radius is 90°.

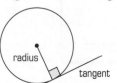

## Exercise S1

**1** Two shapes fit together to make a right-angled triangle.
Find the size of angles *a*, *b* and *c*.

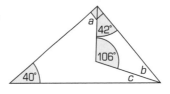

**2** Calculate angles *a*, *b*, *c* and *d*.

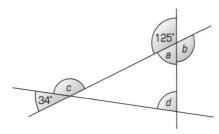

Explain how you found each angle.

**3** Angie draws a parallelogram.
Calculate the angles *x* and *y*.

**4** ABCD is a rectangle.

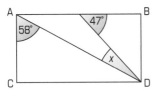

Find angle *x*.
Explain how you found your answer.

**5** This star has rotational symmetry order 5.
Find angles *x* and *y*.

**6** This pattern has rotational symmetry order 5.
  **a** What is the size of angle *y*?
     Show your working.
     Each quadrilateral shown in the diagram is made
     from two congruent (identical) isosceles triangles.
  **b** What is the special name of this quadrilateral?
  **c** Work out the size of angle *z*.

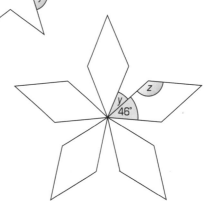

**7** A rectangle is shown resting on a triangle.
Find angle *x*.

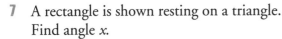

**8** Angle RPQ = 35°.
Explain why angle PRQ = 55°.

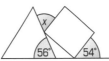

**9** A is the centre of the circle.

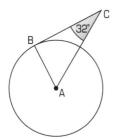

BC is a tangent to the circle at B.
Angle ACB = 32°.
Find angle CAB.

▶ A polygon is a closed shape with three or more straight sides.

Pentagon

Hexagon

Octagon

An **exterior angle** of a polygon is formed by extending one of the sides.

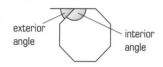

Regular polygons have equal angles and sides.

You should learn these polygon angle facts:

▷ The sum of the exterior angles of any polygon is 360°.
▷ An exterior angle of a regular $n$-sided polygon = 360 ÷ $n$.
▷ An interior angle = 180° − exterior angle.
▷ The sum of the interior angles of a regular $n$-sided polygon = interior angle × $n$.

> **example**
>
> Find the sum of the interior angles of a decagon (a 10-sided polygon).
>
> ............................................................................
>
> Exterior angle = 360 ÷ 10 = 36°
> Interior angle = 180 − 36 = 144°
> Sum interior angles = 144 × 10 = 1440°

You should know these special triangles:

Right-angled
One 90° angle

Isosceles
Two angles equal

Equilateral
All three angles equal

You should know these special quadrilaterals:

Trapezium
One pair of parallel sides

Parallelogram
Two pairs of parallel sides

Rhombus
All sides equal

> **example**
>
> ABDE is a trapezium and BCD is an isoseles triangle.
>
>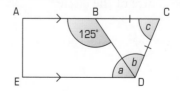
>
> Find angles $a$, $b$, and $c$.
>
> .........................................................................
>
> Angle CBD = 55° (angles on a straight line)
>       $a$ = 55° (alternate angles)
>       $b$ = 55° (isosceles triangle)
>       $c$ = 70° (angles on a triangle)

1 This is an isosceles triangle.

    **a** If angle $x = 24°$, work out angle $y$.
    **b** If angle $y = 24°$, work out angle $x$.

2 A heptagon can be split into 5 triangles.

    **a** Explain how you know the angles inside a heptagon add up to 900°.

    **b** What do the angles inside a pentagon add up to?
      Explain how you know.

    **c** What do the angles inside an octagon add up to?

3 The angles inside a dodecagon add up to 1800°.

    **a** Work out the size of one interior angle inside a regular dodecagon.
    **b** Work out the size of one exterior angle on a regular dodecagon.

4 Here is a parallelogram.

    **a** What would you change on the parallelogram to turn it into a rhombus?
    **b** What would you change on the parallelogram to turn it into a rectangle?

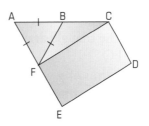

5 The diagram shows an equilateral triangle ABF.
  CDEF is a rectangle.
  ABC and AFE are straight lines.
  Show that BCF is an isosceles triangle.

6 A quadrilateral has opposite sides the same length.
  Write down other facts that will mean the quadrilateral has to be a square.

7 PQR and PRS are isosceles triangles on
  the same base PR.
  Angle PQR = 24° and angle PRS = 96°.
  Show that angle QPS = 36°.

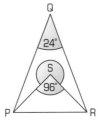

8 ABCD is a rhombus.
  Angle ABC = $3x$, angle BCD = $2x$.
  Find $x$.

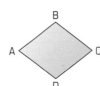

9 Jenny has two shapes of tiles. One is an octagon
  and one is an equilateral triangle.
  The side length of each tile is the same.
  Jenny says the tiles will fit like this.
  Show calculations to prove that Jenny is wrong.

**L6** 1 The shape has **3 identical white** tiles and
**3 identical blue** tiles.
The sides of each tile are all the same length.
Opposite sides of each tile are parallel.
One of the angles is 70°.
**a** Calculate the size of **angle k.**
**b** Calculate the size of **angle m.**
Show your working.

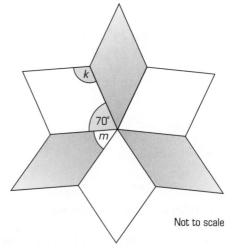

Not to scale

**S1**

2 The diagram shows two isosceles triangles inside
a parallelogram.
**a** On a copy of the diagram, mark another
angle that is 75°.
Label it 75°.
**b** Calculate the size of the angle marked k.
Show your working.

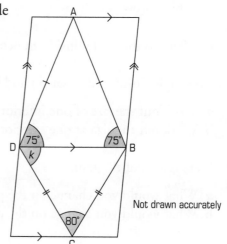

Not drawn accurately

**S1**

Now look at the triangle drawn on the
straight line PQ.
**c** Write x in terms of y.
**d** Now write x in terms of t and w.
**e** Use your answers to parts (c) and (d) to
show that $y = t + w$.

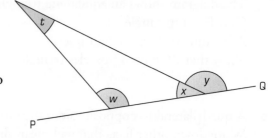

**L7** 3 Here are six different equations, labelled A to F.
Think about the graphs of these equations.
**a** Which graph goes through the point **(0, 0)**?
**b** Which graph is **parallel** to the y-axis?
**c** Which graph is **not** a **straight line**?
**d** Which **two** graphs pass through the point **(3, 7)**?

**A6**

| A | $y = 3x - 4$ | B | $y = 4$ | C | $x = {}^-5$ |
|---|---|---|---|---|---|
| D | $x + y = 10$ | E | $y = 2x + 1$ | F | $y = x^2$ |

**e** The diagram shows the graph of the equation $y = 4 - x^2$.
What are the coordinates of the points where the graph of
this equation meets the graph of equation **E**?

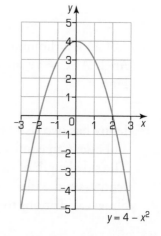

$y = 4 - x^2$

**L7**

**A8**

4   Look at the graph.

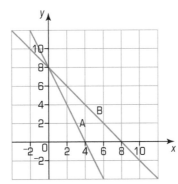

   **a** Show that the equation of line **A** is $2x + y = 8$.
   **b** Write the equation of line **B**.
   **c** On a copy of the graph, draw the line whose equation is $y = 2x + 1$.
      Label your line **C**.
   **d** Solve these simultaneous equations.
      $$y = 2x + 1$$
      $$3y = 4x + 6$$
   Show your working.

**L8**

**A6**

5   Look at this octagon:

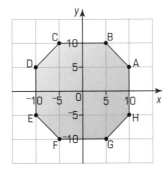

   **a** The line through A and H has the equation $x = 10$.
      What is the equation of the line through **F** and **G**?
   **b** Copy and complete the sentence.
      $x + y = 15$ is the equation of the line through .................... and ..................
   **c** The octagon has four lines of symmetry.
      One of the lines of symmetry has the equation $y = x$.
      On a copy of the diagram, draw and label the line $y = x$.
   **d** The octagon has three **other** lines of symmetry.
      Write the equation of **one** of these three **other** lines of symmetry.
   **e** The line through D and B has the equation $3y = x + 25$.
      The line through G and H has the equation $x = y + 15$.
      Solve the simultaneous equations
      $$3y = x + 25$$
      $$x = y + 15$$
      Show your working.
   **f** Copy and complete this sentence:
      The line through D and B meets the line through G and H at ( ..........., ............ )

6   Look at the diagram.
   Side AB is the same length as side AC.
   Side BD is the same length as side BC.
   Calculate the value of $x$.
   Show your working.

**S2**

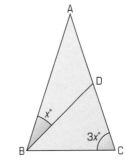

**Pythagoras' theorem** can help you work out the lengths of sides in right-angled triangles.

▶ In a right-angled triangle with sides $a$, $b$, $c$ where $c$ is the hypotenuse:

$$a^2 + b^2 = c^2$$

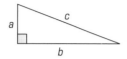

The **hypotenuse** is the longest side.
It is opposite the right angle.

▷ To find the hypotenuse: square the other two sides, add them and then take the square root.
▷ To find a shorter side: square the other two sides, subtract and then take the square root.

*example*

Use Pythagoras' theorem to show that angle $x = 90°$.

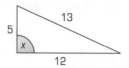

$5^2 + 12^2 = 25 + 144 = 169 = 13^2$
Pythagoras' theorem holds, so the triangle must have a right angle opposite the longest side, that is $x = 90°$.

*example*

**a** Find length PR.
**b** Find length RS.

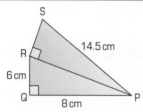

**a** You are looking for the hypotenuse in triangle PQR.
Square the shorter sides and <u>add</u>: $6^2 + 8^2 = 36 + 64 = 100$.
Then take the square root: $\sqrt{100} = 10$ cm, so PR = 10 cm.
**b** You are looking for a shorter side in triangle PRS.
Square the other sides and subtract:
$14.5^2 - 10^2 = 210.25 - 100 = \underline{110.25}$.
Then take the square root: $\sqrt{110.25} = 10.5$, so RS = 10.5 cm.

You can use Pythagoras' theorem to solve real-life problems.

*example*

A 'sleeping policeman' slows traffic down on the roads.
The sleeping policeman must not be higher than 12 cm.
The diagram shows a sleeping policeman from the side.
Is the sleeping policeman too high?

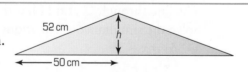

You are looking for a shorter side in the triangle.
Square the other sides and subtract: $52^2 - 50^2 = 2704 - 2500 = 204$.
Then take the square root: $\sqrt{204} = 14.3$ cm.
So the sleeping policeman is too high.

# Exercise S3

  **1** ABD and BCD are right-angled triangles.

    **a** Explain why BD = 15 cm.
    **b** Calculate length AD.

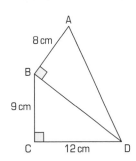

 **2** Calculate the missing length in this right-angled triangle.

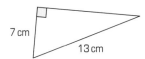

 **3** The diagram shows a ramp.
The ramp is 15 m long and must be at most 1 m high.
What is the least amount of horizontal ground needed?

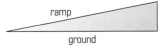

 **4** Explain why angle *x* must be 90°.

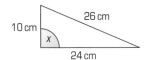

 **5** A free-standing shelving system is kept rigid by a brace.
The brace is positioned diagonally from top to bottom.
What is the length of the brace?

  **6** Two right-angled triangles are joined together to make a larger right-angled triangle.
    **a** Find the perimeter of triangle STU.
    **b** Show that triangle STU is also right-angled.

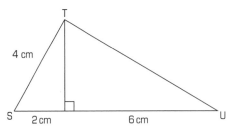

 **7** Beth lives 3.2 km due North of Amy and 4.8 km due West of Cathy.

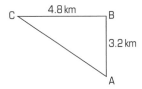

Calculate the direct distance that Amy is from Cathy.

 **8** This a cone.
It has a slant height of 8 cm and perpendicular height 7 cm.
Find the radius of the base of the cone.

> Hint: Use Pythagoras' theorem

45

You use sine, cosine and tangent ratios to find unknown sides and angles in right-angled triangles.

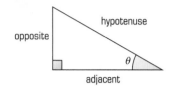

**KEYWORDS**

Sine                    Tangent
Hypotenuse              Opposite
Cosine                  Adjacent
Right-angled triangle

$$\text{sine } \theta = \frac{\text{opposite}}{\text{hypotenuse}} \qquad \text{cosine } \theta = \frac{\text{adjacent}}{\text{hypotenuse}} \qquad \text{tangent } \theta = \frac{\text{opposite}}{\text{adjacent}}$$

These ratios can be abbreviated:

▶ $\sin \theta = \frac{\text{opp}}{\text{hyp}} \qquad \cos \theta = \frac{\text{adj}}{\text{hyp}} \qquad \tan \theta = \frac{\text{opp}}{\text{adj}}$

Follow these steps when using sin, cos or tan:

▷ Label the angle you know or want to find.
▷ Label the sides opposite and adjacent according to the angle; the hypotenuse is always opposite the right angle.
▷ Decide which two sides are involved and then choose the ratio (sin, cos or tan) that connects the two sides.
  ▷ To find a shorter side, multiply by the ratio.
  ▷ To find the hypotenuse, divide by the ratio.
  ▷ To find an angle, divide the sides and use inverse ratio.

**example**

Find the side or angle marked with a letter.

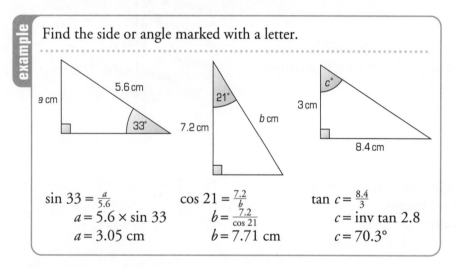

$$\sin 33 = \frac{a}{5.6}$$
$$a = 5.6 \times \sin 33$$
$$a = 3.05 \text{ cm}$$

$$\cos 21 = \frac{7.2}{b}$$
$$b = \frac{7.2}{\cos 21}$$
$$b = 7.71 \text{ cm}$$

$$\tan c = \frac{8.4}{3}$$
$$c = \text{inv tan } 2.8$$
$$c = 70.3°$$

On some calculators you can type in the calculation as it is written, on others to input sin 33 you have to type 33 sin.

You can use trigonometry to solve problems.

**example**

A road sign shows the gradient of a hill as 12.5%.
12.5% as a fraction is $\frac{12.5}{100} = \frac{1}{8}$.
So the hill rises one unit for every 8 horizontal units.
Find the angle of the slope.

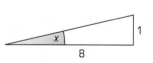

$$\tan x = \frac{1}{8}$$
$$x = \text{inv tan } \frac{1}{8} = 7.1°$$

## Exercise S4

**18** 🖩 **1** Calculate the length $y$.

18 cm

$y$

28°

🖩 **2** Calculate the angle $x$.

15 cm

$x$

4 cm

🖩 **3** Beth lives 3.2 km due North of Amy and 4.8 km due West of Cathy.

C    4.8 km    B

3.2 km

A

Bearings are given as 3 digits measured clockwise from the North line.

    **a** Calculate the bearing of Amy from Cathy.
    **b** Calculate the bearing of Cathy from Amy.
    Give your answers to the nearest degree.

🖩 **4** By how many degrees is angle $q$ bigger than angle $r$?

5 cm

5 cm

$r$

$q$

12 cm

🖩 **5** A right-angled triangle has sides with lengths 20 cm, 21 cm and 29 cm. Calculate the size of the smallest angle in the triangle.

🖩 **6 a** Use the sine ratio to find an expression for the vertical height of this triangle.
    **b** What is the value of $a$ if the area of the triangle is $2x$ cm$^2$? Give your answer to 1 d.p.

$x$ cm

$a$

6 cm

Area of triangle $= \frac{1}{2} \times$ base $\times$ height.

🖩 **7** A rhombus has sides length 6 cm.
    The shorter diagonal is 8 cm long.
    Calculate the size of the angles in the rhombus.

🖩 **8** A diagonal brace is fitted to a square wire frame with side length 80 cm.
    Write down the angle that the brace makes with one side of the square.

80 cm

🖩 **9** A tent pole 1 m tall is secured with ropes 2.4 m in length from the top of the pole to the ground.
    Find the angle the the rope makes with the ground.

1 m   2.4 m

🖩 **10** John looks up to the top of a tree.
    He measures the angle of elevation as 56° and is standing 24 m from the tree.
    John is 1.62 m tall.
    Find an estimate of the height of the tree.

not drawn to scale

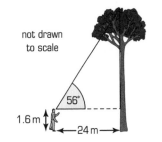

56°

1.6 m

24 m

▶ Shapes are **similar** if their angles are the same and their sides are in the same ratio.

**KEYWORDS**
Congruent          Similar

All equilateral triangles are similar.

**example**

These shapes are similar.
Find side *x*.

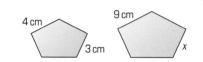

Side *x* corresponds to side of length 3 cm.
The side of length 9 cm corresponds to the side of length 4 cm.
So $\frac{x}{3} = \frac{9}{4}$, rearranging gives $x = \frac{9 \times 3}{4}$
So $x = 6.75$ cm

**example**

Triangles ABC and BCD are similar.
What is the length of AC?

Corresponding sides are in the same ratio:

$\frac{AC}{4.4} = \frac{6.8}{3.74}$

So AC = $6.8 \div 3.74 \times 4.4 = 8$ cm

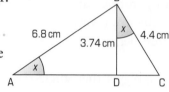

▶ Shapes are **congruent** if their angles and their sides are exactly the same.

**example**

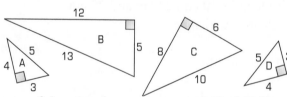

**a** Which two of the triangles are congruent? Explain how you know.

**b** Which two of the shapes are mathematically similar, but not congruent? Explain how you know.

**a** A and D; corresponding sides are equal

**b** A and C (or C and D); corresponding sides are in the same ratio

**example**

This quadrilateral is made from two congruent isosceles triangles.
Find angle *x*.

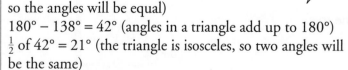

$360° - 84° = 276°$ (angles at a point add up to 360°)
$\frac{1}{2}$ of 276° = 138° (the triangles are congruent, so the angles will be equal)
$180° - 138° = 42°$ (angles in a triangle add up to 180°)
$\frac{1}{2}$ of 42° = 21° (the triangle is isosceles, so two angles will be the same)
$x = 21°$

# Exercise S5

**1** The triangles PQR and XYZ are congruent.
What is the length of side XY?

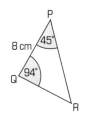

**2** This star shape is made from four congruent isosceles triangles
with a square at its centre.
Find the angle marked *a*.
Explain how you found your answer.

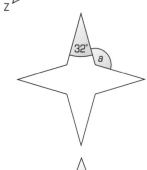

**3** This arrowhead is made of two congruent isosceles triangles.
What is the size of angle *a*?
You must show your working.

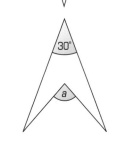

**4** In the diagram, XY is parallel to PQ.
Calculate XY using similar triangles.

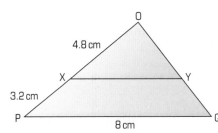

**5** Triangles ABC and DAC are similar.
What is the length of CD?

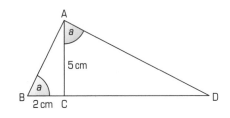

**6** A photograph is placed in a frame.

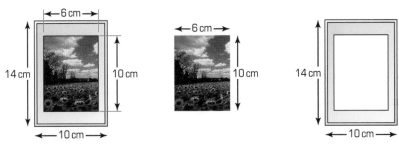

**a** Show that the photograph and the frame are not mathematically similar.

Suppose you wanted a frame that was mathematically similar to the size of the photograph.

**b** Keeping the width of the frame as 10 cm, find the length of the frame.

**7** Are these triangles similar? Explain.

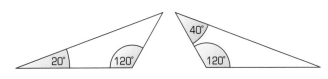

▶ When you reflect, rotate or translate an object, the image will be congruent (same size and shape).

▶ In a **reflection**, the image is on the opposite side of the mirror line.

An object and its image are the same distance away from the mirror line.

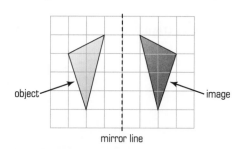

The mirror line is also called the axis of symmetry.

▶ In a **rotation**, an object is rotated about a centre point through an angle (anticlockwise is positive).

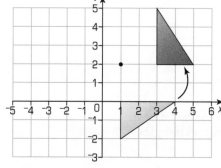

The blue triangle has been rotated through 90° anticlockwise with centre (1, 2).

Use tracing paper to rotate a shape. Keep the centre point in place with the point of a pencil.

▶ In a **translation**, every point of an object moves the same distance and direction.

The blue triangle has been translated through $\begin{pmatrix} 4 \\ 3 \end{pmatrix}$.

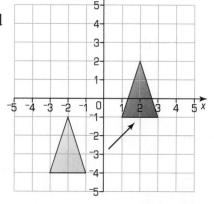

A translation $\begin{pmatrix} -5 \\ -2 \end{pmatrix}$ means 5 units to the left and 2 down.

This is 4 units to the right and 3 units up.

▶ In an **enlargement**, the lengths of the sides of the image are multiplied by the scale factor.

▶ The distance of the image from the centre of enlargement is the scale factor times the distance of the object from the centre of enlargement.

▶ The image is a different size, but the same shape.

The blue triangle has been enlarged with scale factor 2 with centre of enlargement (0, 0).

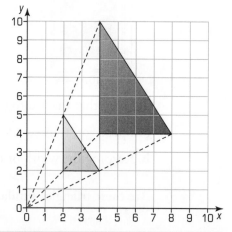

A scale factor of $\frac{1}{2}$ means that the lengths on the image are half those on the object.

# Exercise S6

**L6**

1. On a copy of the grid, draw an enlargement of the arrowhead with scale factor 2.
   Use point C as the centre of enlargement.

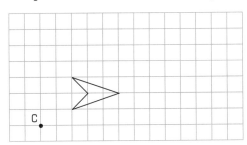

2. On the diagram, the large T-shape is an enlargement of the smaller T-shape.
   What is the scale factor of the enlargement?
   Write down the coordinates of the centre of enlargement.

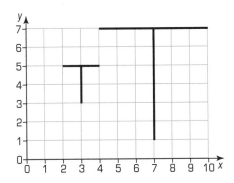

**L7** 

3. A picture of a cat measures 8 cm wide by 4.5 cm high.
   **a** The picture is to be enlarged so that it just fits inside a rectangle
   that measures 18 cm wide by 9 cm.
   By what scale factor should the original picture be enlarged?
   **b** The picture is used so that it just fits onto a badge.
   The badge is 3 cm by 1.5 cm.
   By what scale factor was the original picture multiplied?

4. The larger arrow is an enlargement of the smaller arrow.
   The scale factor of the enlargement is 2.5.
   Write down the values of $a$, $b$ and $c$.

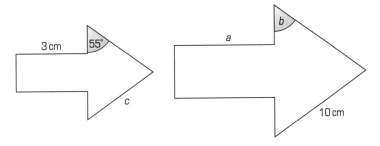

5. Two rectangles are drawn so that one is an enlargement of the other.
   The smaller rectangle has side lengths 2 cm by 7 cm.
   One side of the larger rectangle is 28 cm.
   What are the possible scale factors of the enlargement?

▶ A **net** is a 2-D arrangement that can be folded to form a solid shape.

You should know the nets of these shapes:

**KEYWORDS**
Cuboid                Cone
Regular tetrahedron
Square-based pyramid
Triangular prism

| Cuboid | Regular tetrahedron | Square-based pyramid | Triangular prism |
|---|---|---|---|

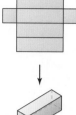  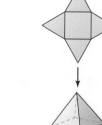 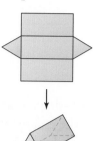

**example**

This net folds to make a tetrahedron.

**a** Which edge will meet the edge AB when folded?

**b** Which corner will meet with corner D when folded?

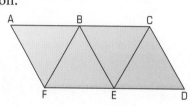

You can use the net of a shape to find its surface area (see S11).

Imagine the net being folded:

**a** The edge AB will meet with the edge BC.

**b** Corner D will meet with corner F.

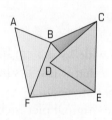

**example**

Name the solid that this is a net of.

The sector of the circle is curled round to make a cone.

▶ **Plans** and **elevations** are projections of a 3-D solid onto a 2-D surface.
  ▷ A **plan view** of a solid is the view from directly overhead (bird's-eye view).
  ▷ An **elevation** is the view from the front or the side of a solid.

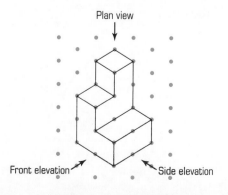

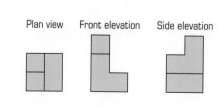

## Exercise S7

**L6**

**1** This net is folded to make a cube.
Copy the net.
  **a** Put a tick on the edge that joins the edge marked with an arrow.
  **b** Put a cross inside the face that will be opposite the shaded face.

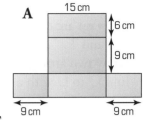

**2** This is a picture of a strawberry box.
It is a box with no lid.
Which of the following nets could fold
to make the strawberry box?

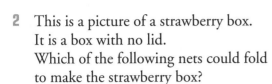

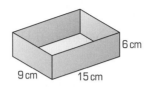

**A**

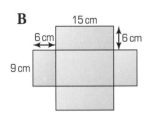

**B**      **C**      **D**      **E**

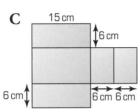 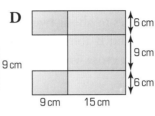 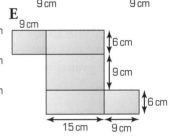

**3** The diagram shows a model made from 11 cubes.

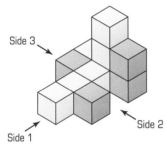

Side 3

Side 1

Side 2

  **a** The drawings below show different side views of the model.
  Which side view does each drawing show?

  **i**           **ii**          **iii**

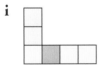      

  **b** Draw the top view of the model.

**4** Tim made a solid letter T using 6 cubes.
He drew a picture of the T on an isometric grid.
He did not draw any side he could not see.
He rotated the solid through 180° so that it was upside-down.
Draw on isometric paper what the solid will look like.

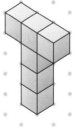

**L7**

**5** The diagram shows an incomplete drawing of a solid cube.
Add 3 straight lines to the diagram to complete the drawing.

**6** Here is a net of a cone.
The cone has radius 4 cm.
Calculate the height of the cone.

  **Hint**: Use Pythagoras' theorem.

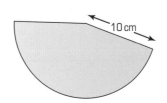

You should know how to do these constructions using a ruler and compasses.

**KEYWORDS**

Compasses        Locus
Bisect             Arc
Perpendicular

To bisect angle PQR:

▷ Draw an arc centred at Q that crosses PQ and QR at S and T.
▷ Draw two arcs centred at S and T that meet at U.
▷ Join Q to U with a straight line.

Bisect means split into two equal parts.

To construct the perpendicular bisector of line AB:

▷ Set the radius of the compasses to about two-thirds the length of AB.
▷ Draw two arcs centred at A and B above and below the line.
▷ Join the points where the arcs cross with a line.

Always leave the construction lines.

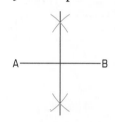

Perpendicular means at right angles to.

To construct a perpendicular from a point X *to* a line YZ:

▷ At X draw arcs cutting line YZ in two places A and B.
▷ Draw the perpendicular bisector of AB.

To construct a perpendicular from a point V *on* a line YZ:

▷ Draw an arc centred at V that cuts the line YZ in two places A and B.
▷ Draw the perpendicular bisector of AB.

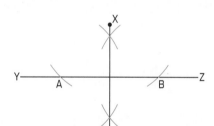

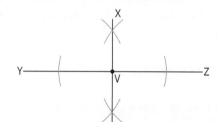

To construct a triangle given all three sides, *x*, *y* and *z*:

▷ Draw a line, PQ, length *x*.
▷ Draw an arc centred at P with radius *y*.
▷ Draw an arc centred at Q with radius *z*.
▷ Join the point where the arcs cross to P and Q.

If you construct an equilateral triangle you also construct an angle of 60°.

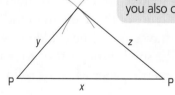

example

Construct a right-angled triangle with shorter sides of length 3 cm and 4 cm.

Draw one of the shorter sides, say the 4 cm side.
Construct a perpendicular from one end of the line.
Measure 3 cm along the perpendicular.
Join the sides to form a triangle.

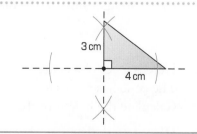

▶ The locus of all points equidistant from a point is a circle.

Equidistant means equal distance.

# Exercise S8

**1** Construct two different isosceles triangles.
Each triangle must have one side 4 cm and one side 7 cm long.

**2** Construct a rhombus with sides of length 5 cm.

**3** A triangle has an area of 12 cm².
One side of the triangle is 8 cm.

  **a** If the triangle is also a right-angled triangle, construct the triangle.
  **b** If the triangle is to be isosceles, construct the triangle.

**4** **a** Construct a right-angled triangle with shorter sides 4 cm and 6 cm.
  **b** Measure the hypotenuse of your triangle.
  **c** Use Pythagoras' theorem to check the accuracy of your drawing and measuring.

**5** The diagram shows two points P and Q.
The locus of all points that are the same distance from P and Q is a straight line.
Construct this line.

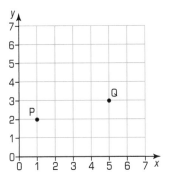

**6** X and Y mark the positions of two villages, 10 km apart.

A mobile phone mast is to be built greater than 4 km from X.
It is to be built closer to X than it is to Y.

Copy the diagram and show the area where the mobile phone mast can be placed.

X •                                                        • Y

Scale 1 cm : 1 km

**7** Joe wants to plant a tree in his back garden.
The tree must be at least 20 m away from the back of the house.
There is a circular pond in the garden, 30 m from the house.
The tree must be at least 5 m away from the pond.

Draw a diagram on a scale of 2 cm to 1 m.
On your diagram show the region in which Joe could plant his tree.

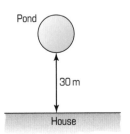

**8** A dog is left outside a shop tied to a horizontal pole 2 m long.
The dog's lead is 1.25 m long.
Draw a diagram showing an accurate construction of the area the dog can reach.
Use a scale 1 cm : 0.5 m.

**L6**

**1** Julie has written a computer program to transform pictures of tiles.
There are **only two instructions** in her program,
**Reflect vertical**
or
**Rotate 90° clockwise.**

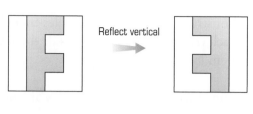

Reflect vertical

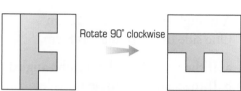

Rotate 90° clockwise

**S6**

**a** Julie wants to transform the first pattern to the second pattern.
Copy and complete the instructions to transform the tiles B1 and B2.
You must use only **Reflect vertical** or **Rotate 90° clockwise**.

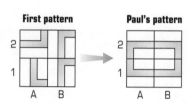

First pattern → Second pattern

**A1** *Tile is in the correct position.*
**A2** *Reflect vertical, and then Rotate 90° clockwise.*
**B1** *Rotate 90° clockwise, and then* ...............................................
**B2** .........................................................................................

**b** Paul starts with the first pattern that was on the screen.
Copy and complete the instructions for the transformations of A2, B1 and B2 to make Paul's pattern.
You must use only **Reflect vertical** or **Rotate 90° clockwise**.

First pattern → Paul's pattern

**A1** *Reflect vertical, and then Rotate 90° clockwise.*
**A2** *Rotate 90° clockwise, and then* ....................
**B1** .........................................................................
**B2** .........................................................................

**2** Four cubes join to make an L-shape.
The diagram shows the L-shape after **quarter turns** in one direction.

**S7**

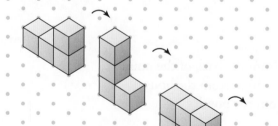

Copy the diagram on an isometric grid.
Draw the L-shape after the **next** quarter turn in the same direction.

**L7**

**3**  **a** Calculate the length of the unknown side of this
right-angled triangle.
Show your working.

**S3**

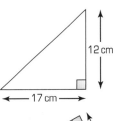

**b** Calculate the length of the unknown side of this
right-angled triangle.
Show your working.

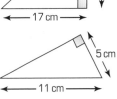

**4**  In the scale drawing, the shaded area represents a lawn.

**S8**

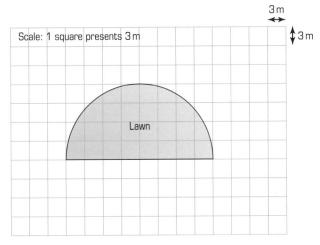

There is a wire fence **all around** the lawn.
The shortest distance from the fence to the edge of the lawn is **always 6 m**.
On a copy of the diagram, draw **accurately** the position of the fence.

**L8**

**5**  A boat sails from the harbour to the buoy.
The buoy is 6 km to the east and 4 km to the north of the harbour.

**S4**

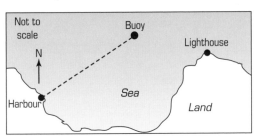

**a** **Calculate** the shortest distance between the buoy and the harbour.
Give your answer to 1 decimal place.
Show your working.
**b** **Calculate** the bearing of the buoy from the harbour.
Show your working.

The buoy is 1.2 km to the north of the lighthouse.
The shortest distance from the lighthouse to the buoy is 2.5 km.
**c** **Calculate** how far the buoy is to the west of the lighthouse.
Give your answer to 1 decimal place.
Show your working.

▶ The perimeter, $P$, is the total distance around a flat shape.

▶ The area, $A$, is the amount of space inside a flat shape.

You should know how to find the area of these shapes.

Rectangle

Triangle

Parallelogram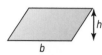

Trapezium

$A = b \times h$

$A = \frac{1}{2} \times b \times h$

$A = b \times h$

$A = \frac{1}{2}(a + b) \times h$

You may have to find the perimeter or area of compound shapes.

Height, $h$, is always perpendicular to base, $b$.

**example**

For this shape, find:    **a** the perimeter    **b** the area.

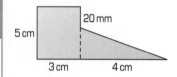

All measurements should be in the same units.

**a**    The vertical height of the triangle is $5 - 2 = 3$ cm
($20$ mm $= 2$ cm).
The hypotenuse $= \sqrt{3^2 + 4^2} = 5$ cm
So the perimeter $= 4 + 3 + 5 + 3 + 2 + 5 = 22$ cm
**b**    Area rectangle $= 5 \times 3 = 15$      Area triangle $= \frac{1}{2} \times 4 \times 3 = 6$
So the total area $= 15 + 6 = 21$ cm$^2$

Use Pythagoras' theorem to find the hypotenuse.

**example**

A square has an area of $64$ mm$^2$. What is its perimeter?

One side of the square $= \sqrt{64} = 8$ mm
So the perimeter $= 4 \times 8 = 32$ mm$^2$

**example**

One side of a rectangle is $n$ cm long. The other side of the
rectangle is $4$ cm long.
Write expressions for:    **a** the area    **b** the perimeter.

**a**    $A = 4 \times n$ or $A = 4n$
**b**    $P = 2 \times (n + 4) = 2n + 8$

**example**

The area of a trapezium is $33.35$ cm$^2$.
Find the distance between the parallel
sides.

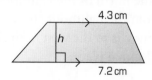

Substitute $A = 33.35$ cm$^2$, $a = 7.2$ cm and $b = 4.3$ cm into the
formula for the area of a trapezium:
$\frac{1}{2}(7.2 + 4.3) \times h = 33.35$
So $h = 33.35 \div 5.75 = 5.8$ cm

# Exercise S9

**1** X, Y and Z are all squares. X has a perimeter of 30 cm.
Y has an area of 30 cm². Z has one side with length 30 cm.
Put X, Y and Z in order of size, smallest to largest.
Show calculations to explain how you worked out your answer.

**2** Each shape below has an area of 54 cm².
Find the height of each shape

**a**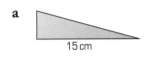
15 cm

**b**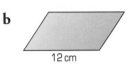
12 cm

**c**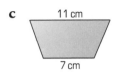
11 cm
7 cm

**3** The diagram shows a 23 cm by 14 cm rectangle.
It has been split into four smaller rectangles.
**a** Work out the area of each of the four smaller rectangles.
**b** Use your answers to part **a** to work out 23 × 14.
Explain why you can do this.

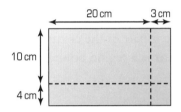
20 cm    3 cm
10 cm
4 cm

**4** What is the area and perimeter of these shapes?
Show your working.

**a**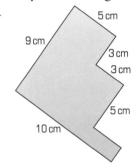
5 cm
9 cm
3 cm
3 cm
5 cm
10 cm

**b**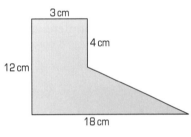
3 cm
4 cm
12 cm
18 cm

**5** A swimming pool measures 12 m by 25 m.
There is a path around the pool 1.8 m wide.
Calculate the area of the path.

**6** This tabletop is in the shape of an isosceles trapezium.
Calculate the area of the tabletop.

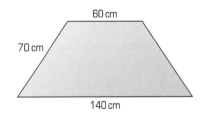
60 cm
70 cm
140 cm

**7** What is the difference, in metres, between 50 miles and 50 km?

**8** A brand of dog food is sold in square tins.
The area of the top of the tin is 25 cm².
A label that goes around the sides of the tin overlaps by 1 cm.
The width of the label is the same as the height of the tin.
The label has an area of 126 cm².
Work out the height of the tin.

**9** An isosceles triangle has base length 8 cm and one angle of 40°.

**a** Calculate the area of the triangle.

**Hint**: Use trigonometry to find the height of the triangle.

**b** Calculate the perimeter of the triangle.

40°
8 cm

**10** Calculate the area of an equilateral triangle with sides of length 6 cm.

► A **circle** is a set of points equidistant from a centre point.
► The **circumference**, *C*, is the distance around the circle.
► The **radius**, *r*, is the distance from the centre to the circumference.
► The **diameter**, *d*, is the distance across the circle through the centre.

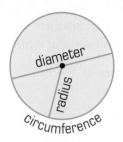

**KEYWORDS**

| | |
|---|---|
| Arc | Chord |
| Sector | Segment |
| Radius | Diameter |
| Circumference | Radius |

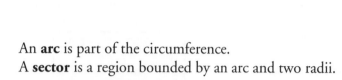

An **arc** is part of the circumference.
A **sector** is a region bounded by an arc and two radii.

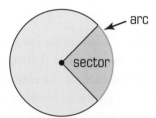

A **chord** joins two points on the circumference.
It divides a circle into two **segments**.

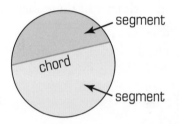

You should know these circle formulae:

► Circumference, $C = 2 \times \pi \times r = \pi \times d$

► Area, $A = \pi \times r^2$

Use the $\pi$ button on your calculator or use $\pi = \frac{22}{7}$ or $\pi = 3.142$.

---

**example**

Find the circumference and area of a circle with radius 5 cm.

..................................................................................................

$C = 2 \times \pi \times 5 = 31.4$ cm
$A = \pi \times 5^2 = 78.5$ cm$^2$

---

Arc length $= \frac{\theta}{360} \times C$
Sector area $= \frac{\theta}{360} \times A$,
where $\theta$ is the angle at the centre.

> Arc length and sector area are fractions of circumference and area.

---

**example**

**a** Which sector has the biggest area, A or B?
**b** What is the perimeter of sector A?

..................................................................................................

**a** Area A $= \frac{1}{4} \times \pi \times 4^2 = 12.6$ cm$^2$;
   area B $= \frac{1}{3} \times \pi \times 3^2 = 9.4$ cm$^2$
   So area A is greater than area B.
**b** Perimeter A $= \frac{1}{4} \times 2 \times \pi \times 4 + (4 + 4)$
   $= 14.28$ cm

---

# Exercise S10

**L6** **M** **1** What is the approximate circumference of a circle with diameter 6 cm?

**M** **2** What is the approximate area of a circle with radius 5 cm?

**3** Explain why the largest chord in a circle is the diameter.

**4** A trundle wheel is used to measure distance.
A trundle wheel measures 100 cm with one complete rotation.
What is the radius of the wheel?

**5** Class 9C make a trundle wheel with radius 40 cm.
   **a** What is the circumference of this trundle wheel?
   **b** Class 9C use the wheel to measure the length of the school car park.
   The wheel makes 56 rotations.
   Calculate the length, to the nearest metre, of the school car park.

**6** A circle has a radius of 8 cm. Calculate the area of the circle.

**7** A circle has circumference 80 cm. Calculate the radius of the circle.

**L7** **M** **8** The area, in square centimetres, of a circle is $64\pi$.
What is the radius of the circle?

**9** A tin of beans has diameter 5.2 cm and height 6.8 cm.
The label that wraps around the tin is removed and laid flat.
Calculate the area of the label.

**10** A circle is drawn inside a square.
The circle touches the edges of the square.
The square has side lengths 8 cm.

What fraction of the square does the circle cover?
Show all your working.

**11** A round table has diameter 140 cm.
To sit comfortably at the table a person needs 45 cm around
the circumference.
How many people can sit comfortably around this table?

**12** A circular pond of radius 70 cm is dug in a garden.
There is a path around the pond 1 m wide.
What is the area of the path?

**13** The diagram shows two circles with radii 3 cm and 6 cm.
The smaller circle lies completely inside the larger circle.

Work out the shaded area.

**L8** **14** The diagram shows the sector of a circle.
It is $\frac{1}{6}$ of the whole circle.

Calculate:
   **a** the area of the sector
   **b** the perimeter of the sector.

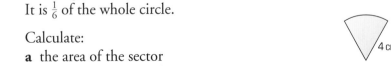

4 cm

61

► The **surface area** is the total area of all surfaces.

To calculate surface area you must have all dimensions given in the same units.

Surface area of a cuboid = $2(l \times w) + 2(w \times h) + 2(h \times l)$

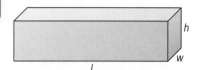

**KEYWORDS**
Surface area     Prism
Cuboid

If the units are different change them so that they are all the same.

To find the surface area of shapes like prisms, find the area of each surface then add the areas.

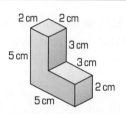

**example**

Find the surface area of this shape.

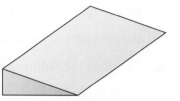

There are four different-shaped faces:
Area of square face = 2 cm × 2 cm = 4 cm$^2$
Area of L-shaped face = 2 cm × 3 cm + 2 cm × 5 cm = 16 cm$^2$
Area of 2 × 5 rectangular face = 2 cm × 5 cm = 10 cm$^2$
Area of 2 × 3 rectangular face = 2 cm × 3 cm = 6 cm$^2$

There are two of each type of face:
Total area = 2(4 cm$^2$ + 16 cm$^2$ + 10 cm$^2$ + 6 cm$^2$) = 36 cm$^2$

► The metric units of area are mm$^2$, cm$^2$, m$^2$ and km$^2$.

You can fit 10 mm × 10 mm = 100 mm$^2$ inside a 1 cm × 1 cm square.

▷ To change cm$^2$ to mm$^2$ multiply by 100.
▷ To change mm$^2$ to cm$^2$ divide by 100.

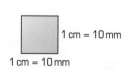
1 cm = 10 mm
1 cm = 10 mm

You can fit 100 cm × 100 cm = 10 000 cm$^2$ inside a 1 m × 1 m square.

▷ To change m$^2$ to cm$^2$ multiply by 10 000.
▷ To change cm$^2$ to m$^2$ divide by 10 000.

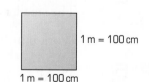
1 m = 100 cm
1 m = 100 cm

**example**

Write:  **a** 42 000 mm$^2$ in cm$^2$  **b** 6.3 m$^2$ in cm$^2$.

**a**  42 000 mm$^2$ ÷ 100 = 420 cm$^2$
**b**  6.3 m$^2$ × 10 000 = 63 000 cm$^2$

## Exercise S11

**1** The diagram shows the net for a cuboid.
Each blue square represents 1 cm squared.
Calculate the surface area of the cuboid.

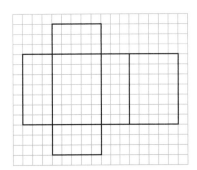

**2** A box of chocolates is made in the shape of a triangular prism.
Calculate the surface area of the box.

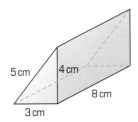

5 cm   4 cm
8 cm
3 cm

 **3** Mosaic tiles are 40 mm by 40 mm.
How many do you need to cover 1 m²?

**4** The surface area of a cuboid is 740 000 cm².
What is the surface area of the cuboid in:   **a** m²   **b** mm²?

 **5** A cube has surface area 240 000 cm².
Write down the length of one side of the cube.

 **6** Calculate the surface area of a cylinder of radius 3.2 cm and
height 8.5 cm.

3.2 cm

8.5 cm

 **7** Calculate the surface area of this wedge.
Give your answer to the nearest integer.

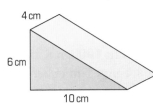

4 cm

6 cm

10 cm

 **8** The surface area of a cuboid is 66 cm².
The cuboid has a pair of squares faces.
The edges of the cuboid are all integer (whole number)
values in cm.
If one edge of the cuboid is 3 cm, what are the lengths
of the other two edges?

 **9** Sydney, a worker bee, stores honey in regular hexagonal
shaped cells.
The diagram shows the shape and size of the front of each cell.

**a** Calculate the surface area of the front of the cell.

Each cell is filled to a depth of 20 mm.

**b** Calculate the total surface area of the whole of one cell.

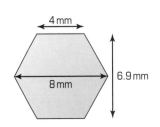

4 mm

8 mm

6.9 mm

▶ **Volume** is the amount of space taken up by an object.

**KEYWORDS**
Volume          Cylinder
Cuboid          Prism

To calculate volume you must have all dimensions in the same units.

▶ Volume of a cuboid = $l \times w \times h$

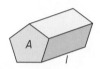

▶ Volume of a prism = $A \times l$

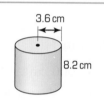

**example**

Find the volume of this cylinder.

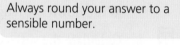

Area of circular end, $A = \pi \times 3.6^2$
Volume = $\pi \times 3.6^2 \times 8.2 = 333.9 \text{ cm}^3$

Always round your answer to a sensible number.

You can fit 10 mm × 10 mm × 10 mm = 1000 mm³ inside a
1 cm × 1 cm × 1 cm cube.

▷ To change cm³ to mm³ multiply by 1000.
▷ To change mm³ to cm³ divide by 1000.

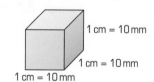

You can fit 100 cm × 100 cm × 100 cm = 1 000 000 cm³ inside a
1 m × 1 m × 1 m cube.

▷ To change m³ to cm³ multiply by 1 000 000.
▷ To change cm³ to m³ divide by 1 000 000.

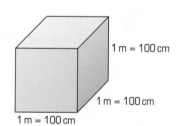

**example**

Cuboid A has length 6 cm, width 4 cm and height 15 cm.
Cuboid B has length 90 mm, width 50 mm and height 80 mm.
Show that the cuboids have the same volume.

Volume of A = $6 \times 4 \times 15 = 360 \text{ cm}^3$
Volume of B = $90 \times 50 \times 80 = 360\ 000 \text{ mm}^3 = 360 \text{ cm}^3 \ (\div 1000)$

# Exercise S12

L6

**1** The diagram shows the net for a cuboid.
The net is folded up to make a cuboid.
Calculate the volume of the cuboid.

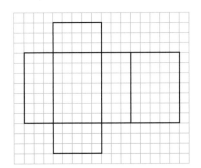

**2** A box of chocolates is made in the shape of a triangular prism.
Calculate the volume of the box.

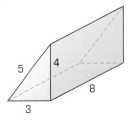

**M** **3** What is the volume of a cuboid measuring 4 cm by 5 cm by 6 cm?

**M** **4** A cube has volume 64 cm³. What is the length of the sides of the cube?

**M** **5** A shape has volume 0.032 m³.
What is its volume in: **a** cm³ **b** mm³?

**6** A seed tray measures 2 m long, 50 cm wide and 18 cm deep.
How much earth will it hold?

**7** These two cuboids have the same volume.

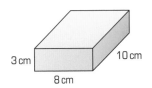

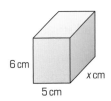

**a** What is the volume of cuboid A? **b** Work out the length marked *x*.

L7  **8** Calculate the volume of a cylinder with radius 6 cm and
height 11 cm.

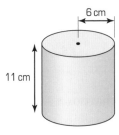

 **9** Calculate the volume of this wedge.
Give your answer to the nearest integer.

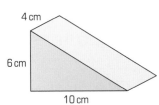

L8  **10** Sydney, a worker bee, stores honey in regular hexagonal shaped cells.
The diagram shows the shape and size of the front of each cell.
Each cell is filled to a depth of 20 mm.
 **a** Calculate the volume of honey that Sydney can store in one cell.
 **b** Work out how many cells are needed to store 10 000 mm³ of
honey.

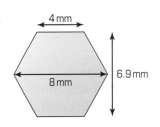

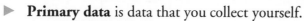

▶ **Primary data** is data that you collect yourself.
▶ **Secondary data** is data that has already been collected.

You can carry out a survey or experiment to collect data.

▷ You need a data collection sheet to record the data you collect.
▷ You need to choose a sample that will not be biased.

A questionnaire is a list of questions used to gather data in a survey.

▷ Use answer boxes that cover all possible answers and do not overlap.

**example**

Ellie carried out a survey to find out how much money students spend in the school canteen each week and what they buy.

Ellie asked 20 of her friends.

**a** Explain why this might not give very good data.

One of Ellie's questions was:

*How much do you usually spend on drinks each week?*

☐ *A lot*    ☐ *A little*    ☐ *Nothing*    ☐ *Don't know*

**b** Explain what is wrong with the choices she has given and write new labels for the boxes.

..........................................................................................

**a** Ellie's friends may all buy the same type of food and may all be girls. This data may be biased.
Ellie should ask boys and girls and students from each school year.

**b** 'A lot' and 'a little' mean different things to different people so you should specify amounts. Make sure that the amounts do not overlap and that there are no gaps so that students can tick only one box. For example:

☐ *Nothing*    ☐ *Less than £5*

☐ *£5–£10*     ☐ *Over £10*

A **pie chart** uses a circle to display data.

▷ The whole pie represents the total frequency,
▷ The angle at the centre of the circle is proportional to the frequency.
▷ $\frac{360°}{\text{total frequency}}$ represents one item.

**example**

Chloe carried out a survey about favourite subjects.
She drew a pie chart to represent the results of her survey.
The sector for Languages represents 12 students.
How many students did Chloe ask in her survey?

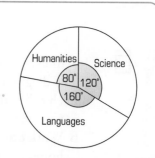

..........................................................................................

160° means 12 pupils.
Therefore 1° means 12 ÷ 160.
So number of students in the survey is 360 × (12 ÷ 160) = 27.

# Exercise D1

**L6**

1   A local council said in its annual report:

   '72% of households recycle their plastic, glass and paper each week.'

   Lexie thought that more households than that recycled plastic, glass and paper.
   She decided to do a survey and asked 24 people who lived in her street.
   Give two different reasons why Lexie's sample might not give very good data.

2   Children in Crayton begin school in September if their birthday is from September to February, and in January if their birthday is from March to August.
   Jenny wants to investigate if more children who go to school earlier, in September, are in the top maths set.
   She decides to ask 16 of her friends in her year group what maths set they are in.

   Give two different ways in which Jenny could improve her survey.

3   Kerry is carrying out a survey to find out how often people have their hair cut.

   **a** Write a question for her survey. (Remember to include answer boxes.)
   **b** What other facts might be important for Kerry to find out in her survey?

 4   Thirty-two out of thirty-six pupils said they watch *The Simpsons*.
   What angle would show this on a pie chart?

5   Class JR were asked to state which sport they preferred to play in games.
   They had to choose between football, hockey and rugby.
   The table shows their preferences.

| Sport | Number |
|-------|--------|
| Football | 5 |
| Hockey | 9 |
| Rugby | 10 |

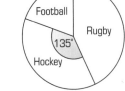

   **a** Draw a pie chart to show this information.
   Show your working and draw your angles accurately.
   **b** Class JB were also asked to state their preferred sport.
   Their preferences are shown in the pie chart.

   The sector for hockey represents 12 pupils.
   How many pupils in total are there in class JB?

6   Eight out of thirty-two boys in a class at a school have blond hair.
   **a** What angle would show this on a pie chart?

   Exactly one-quarter of the boys in this class also have blue eyes.
   **b** From this information what percentage of the boys have blond hair and blue eyes?
   Choose from:

   $6\frac{1}{4}\%$      $12\frac{1}{2}\%$      25%      50%      Not possible to tell

**L7**

7   Rudi drew the pie chart to show how much time, on average, he spends doing things on a school day.

   **a** The sum of the sectors is not 100%.
   Does this mean that there has been a mistake in the pie chart?
   Explain your answer.
   **b** Calculate how much time, on average, Rudi spends watching TV.
   Give your answer in hours and minutes.

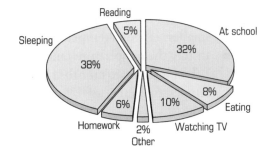

67

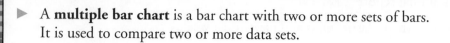

▶ A **multiple bar chart** is a bar chart with two or more sets of bars. It is used to compare two or more data sets.

▶ A **percentage bar chart** shows the total frequency in a single bar. You find the percentage of each category.

**KEYWORDS**
Continuous      Bar chart
Multiple bar chart
Percentage bar chart
Frequency diagram
Time series

The graph shows the different ways teachers travel to work at two schools, X and Y.

**a** About what percentage of teachers at school X travel to work by car?

**b** There are 60 teachers at school X that travel by car. Estimate how many teachers there are in total at school X.

**c** There are 140 teachers at school Y. At which school do more teachers cycle to work?

..................................................................................

**a** 75%

**b** $(60 \times 100) \div 75 = 80$

**c** At X, 15% of 80 = 12 teachers cycle. At Y, 10% of 140 = 14 teachers cycle. More teachers cycle at school Y.

▶ A **frequency diagram** is used to display continuous data. Frequency is given by the height of the rectangles. There are no gaps between the rectangles.

The graph shows the waiting times of 50 customers at a supermarket check out.
Estimate the probability that you will have to wait less than 3 minutes.

.................................................

$p$ (wait less than 3 minutes) $= \frac{(3 + 5 + 12)}{50} = \frac{20}{50} = 0.4$

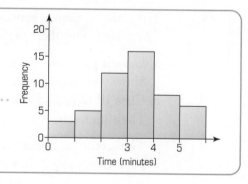

▶ A **time series** shows how something changes over time.
  ▷ Time is always given on the horizontal axis.
  ▷ Points on the graph can be joined to compare trends over time.

The graph shows the maximum and minimum midday temperatures in Paris over the last year.

**a** In which month did Paris have the smallest range in temperature?

**b** In July the temperature range was 7°. Which other two months had a temperature range of 7°?

...........................................

**a** August, as it has the shortest bar

**b** March and September

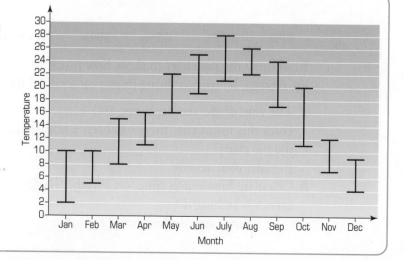

# Exercise D2

**L6**

**1** The bar chart shows the ages of employees in a company.

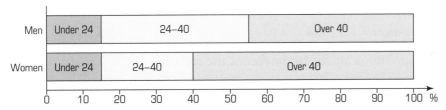

**a** What percentage of men who work for the company are aged 24–40?

**b** There are 15 women aged 24–40 working for the company.
Find the total number of women who work for the company.

**c** Iain says that the same number of men and women under 24 work
for the company.
Explain why he may not be correct.

**2** The graph shows the number
of mature students attending
Townly University.
Use the diagram to decide
whether or not the following
statements are true, false or you
cannot be certain. In each case
explain your answer.

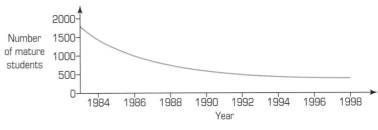

**a** The number of mature students attending Townly University in 2003 was 400.

**b** The number of mature students at Townly University fell by more than two-thirds
from 1984 to 1994.

**c** There were fewer students in total at Townly University in 1996 than in 1990.

**3** The graph shows the temperature, taken at
hourly intervals, of a hospital patient.
**a** Estimate the patient's temperature at
  **i** 7.30 am    **ii** 11.30 am
**b** Explain why your answers in part **a** can
only be estimates.

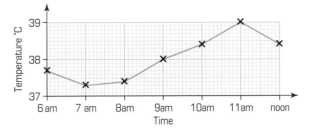

**L7**

**4** The frequency diagram shows times spent on the
telephone one evening by a sample of students.
Nick said most students spent less that 1 hour on
the phone.
Explain why this statement is false.

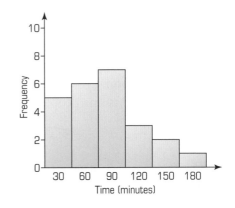

**5** Students in Years 10 and 11 at a school have opted
to study history, geography or both subjects
There are 240 students in each year group.

**a** How many students studied both history and
geography in    **i** Year 10    **ii** Year 11?
**b** How many students in total studied history,
but not geography?

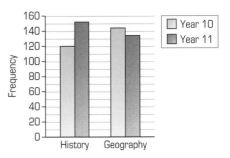

**L6**

1  Jenny and Alan each have a rectangle made out of paper.

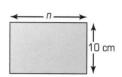

One side is 10 cm.
The other side is $n$ cm.

**a** They write expressions for the **perimeter** of the rectangle.

Jenny writes    $2n + 20$
Alan writes    $2(n + 10)$

Identify the true statement below.

A:  Jenny is correct and Alan is wrong.
B:  Jenny is wrong and Alan is correct.
C:  Both Jenny and Alan are correct.
D:  Both Jenny and Alan are wrong.

**b** Alan cuts his rectangle, then puts the two halves side by side.

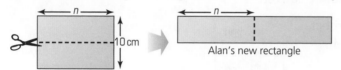

Alan's new rectangle

What is the perimeter of Alan's new rectangle?
Write your expression as simply as possible.

**c** Jenny cuts her rectangle a different way, and puts one half below the other.

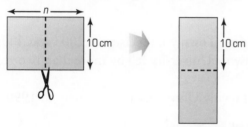

Jenny's new rectangle

What is the perimeter of Jenny's new rectangle?
Write your expression as simply as possible.

**d** What value of $n$ would make the perimeter of Jenny's new rectangle the **same value** as the perimeter of Alan's new rectangle?

**L7**

2  At Winchester there is a large table known as the Round Table of King Arthur.
The **diameter** of the table is **5.5 metres**.

**a** A book claims that 50 people sat around the table.
Assume each person needs 45 cm around the circumference of the table.
Is it possible for 50 people to sit around the table?
Show your working to explain your answer.

**b** Assume people sitting around the table could reach only **1.5 m**.

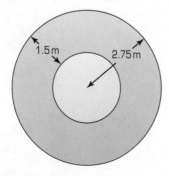

Calculate the **area** of the table that could be reached.
Show your working.

**S9**

**S10**

**L7**

**D1**

3   The pie chart shows how much time **each day**, on average, we spend doing different things.

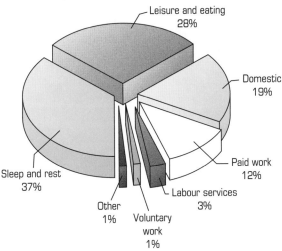

**How Britons use their time (1995 data)**

Leisure and eating
28%

Domestic
19%

Sleep and rest
37%

Paid work
12%

Labour services
3%

Other
1%

Voluntary
work
1%

Data from 'Economic Trends', Office for National Statistics, © Crown Copyright 1998

**a** The sum of the percentages is not 100%.
   Does this mean there must be a mistake in the pie chart?
   Explain your answer.

**b** Calculate how much time in one day (24 hours) we spend on average
   on **paid work**.
   Show your working and give your answer in hours and minutes.

**c** Most days of paid work are at least 7 hours long.
   Give one reason why the average amount is **less** than this.

**L8**

**S12**

4   **a** This solid is a prism, with height $3x$.
      The cross-section is shaded.

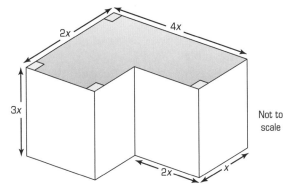

$2x$   $4x$

$3x$

Not to
scale

$2x$   $x$

Write an expression for the **volume** of the solid.
Show your working and simplify your expression.

The volume of this prism is given by the expression $8x^3 \sin a$.

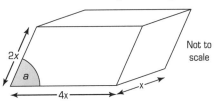

$2x$

$a$

$4x$   $x$

Not to
scale

**b** What value of $a$ would make the volume of the prism $8x^3$?

**c** The prism has a volume of 500 cm³.
   The value of $a$ is 30°.
   What is the value of $x$?
   Show your working.

▶ The **range** represents the spread of the data.
It is the difference between the largest and smallest values in a set of data.

To estimate the range from a grouped frequency table, find the difference between the upper bound of the last class and the lower bound of the first class.

An average is a representative value of a set of data.

▶ A **mode** is a data value that occurs most often. There can be more than one mode.
▶ The **median** is the middle value when the data is arranged in order.
▶ The **mean** is calculated by adding all the data values then dividing by the number of pieces of data. To estimate the mean from a grouped frequency table you use the mid-point of each class.

> **KEYWORDS**
> Assumed mean     Mean
> Estimated mean    Mode
> Median
> Range

**example**

Tom has 4 number cards.
The mean is 7.
Tom is given a fifth card.
What could the number on the fifth card be if:

| 6 | 8 | 9 | 5 |

**a** the mean stays the same     **b** the mean decreases by 1
**c** the mode is 8     **d** the median is 6
**e** the range stays the same?

........................................................................

**a** 7 (total must be 35: $35 \div 5 = 7$)
**b** 2 (total must be 30: $30 \div 5 = 6$)
**c** 8       **d** 6 or less      **e** 5, 6, 7, 8 or 9

**example**

Find the mean number of matches from this frequency table.

| Number of matches | 32 | 33 | 34 | 35 | 36 |
|---|---|---|---|---|---|
| Frequency | 4 | 6 | 12 | 5 | 3 |

Mean = $[(32 \times 4) + (33 \times 6) + (34 \times 12) + (35 \times 5) + (36 \times 3)]$
$\div (4 + 6 + 12 + 5 + 3) = 1017 \div 30 = 33.9$

> You could use an assumed mean.
> Subtract 30 from each number of matches.
> Mean = $[(2 \times 4) + (3 \times 6) + (4 \times 12) + (5 \times 5) + (6 \times 3)] \div 30 = 3.9$
> Add 30 to the answer:
> $30 + 3.9 = 33.9$

**example**

The table shows the speeds of a sample of 120 cars travelling on a motorway.
Estimate the range and mean of this data.

| Speed, $v$ mph | $50 \leqslant v < 60$ | $60 \leqslant v < 70$ | $70 \leqslant v < 80$ | $80 \leqslant v < 90$ | $90 \leqslant v < 100$ |
|---|---|---|---|---|---|
| Frequency | 6 | 21 | 47 | 38 | 8 |

Range = $100 - 50 = 50$
Mean = $[(55 \times 6) + (65 \times 21) + (75 \times 47) + (85 \times 38) + (95 \times 8)] \div (6 + 21 + 47 + 38 + 8)$
$= (330 + 1365 + 3525 + 3230 + 760) \div 120 = 9210 \div 120 = 76.75$ mph

The modal class for this data is $70 \leqslant v < 80$ mph.
The median speed for this data lies in the class $70 \leqslant v < 80$ mph.

## Exercise D3

**L6**

**1** Jenny played two games of tenpin bowling.
Her mean score was 98 and the range of her scores was 6.
What were her scores in each game?

**2** Four number cards are placed face down on a table so that their
numbers are hidden.
The mode of the numbers is 7. The mean of the numbers is 6.
What could be the numbers on each of the four number cards?

**3** Terry has three number cards. The mean of these three numbers is 7.
Terry chooses another card.

a If the mean of the four number cards is still 7, what is the number on the card?
b If the mean of the four numbers goes down by 1, what is the number on the card?

**L7** **M**

**4** The mean of two numbers is 8.
One of the numbers is ⁻2, what is the other number?

**5** The table shows the number of tries scored by a rugby
team in 16 matches one season.

a Show that the total number of tries scored is 36.
b Calculate the mean number of tries per match.

| Number of tries scored | 0 | 1 | 2 | 3 | 4 |
|---|---|---|---|---|---|
| Number of matches | 1 | 3 | 4 | 7 | 1 |

**6** For the whole of one calendar year, a maths set had the same pupils.
The mean and range of their ages at the beginning of that year were:

**mean**: 14 years 3 months     **range**: 10 months 3 days

a What was the mean and range of their ages at the end of that year?
b The mean and range of the ages of another maths set are:

**mean**: 14 years 7 months     **range**: 11 months 12 days

A new pupil whose age is 14 years 7 months joins this maths set.
What effect will this have on the mean age and range of
ages of this maths set?

**7** Helen carried out a survey into waiting times at a health centre.
She drew this graph to display her results.

Calculate an estimate of the mean waiting time.

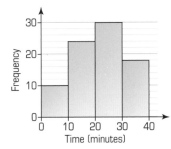

**L8**

**8** The percentage chart shows information about the wingspan
of a sample of bats.
Calculate an estimate of the mean wingspan of this sample of bats.

```
0%        18%              62%           100%   Key:
                                                ▨ 30–50 cm
                                                ▢ 50–80 cm
                                                ▢ 80–120 cm
```

**9** The table shows the arrival time before the start of an exam of a group of 24 girls.

| Arrival time | 0–2 | 2–4 | 4–6 | 6–8 | 8–10 | 10–12 |
|---|---|---|---|---|---|---|
| Frequency | 4 | 9 | 5 | 3 | 2 | 1 |

a Write down the modal class for this data.
b Estimate the range of this data.
c Calcualte an estimate of the mean arrival time for this data.

A **stem-and-leaf diagram** is a way of displaying a small amount of grouped data.

▷ The stem is written to the left of a vertical line, leaves to the right.
▷ Leaves for each stem are ordered.
▷ Always write a key.

**example**

The stem- and leaf-diagram shows the speed of a sample of cars travelling up a hill.
Find: **a** the range **b** the median.

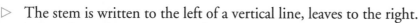

```
6 | 2
5 | 0 1 4 6 7 8 8
4 | 2 5 7 9
3 | 3 6
2 | 8
```

This is the stem.

These are leaves.
They are in order.

Key: 4 | 2 means 42 miles

**a** Range = 62 − 28 = 34
**b** Median is $\frac{15+1}{2}$th value = 50

If you have a large amount of data it can be represented on a cumulative frequency diagram.
You use a cumulative frequency diagram to estimate the median and interquartile range.

▶ The **interquartile range** is the range of the middle 50% of the data.
Interquartile range = upper quartile − lower quartile

The diagram represents the speed of 120 cars travelling on a motorway.

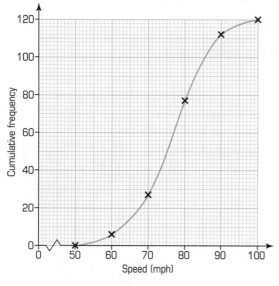

$\frac{1}{2}$ of 120 = 60   Median = 78 mph

$\frac{1}{4}$ of 120 = 30   Lower quartile = 71 mph

$\frac{3}{4}$ of 120 = 90   Upper quartile = 84 mph

You do not need to find the ($n$ + 1)th value when you have a large amount of data.

Interquartile range = upper quartile − lower quartile = 84 − 71 = 13 mph

**example**

Estimate the number of cars that were travelling at speeds greater than 75 mph.

At 75 mph: 46 cars
120 − 46 = 74 cars were travelling faster than 75 mph.

# Exercise D4

**L7** **1** The stem-and-leaf diagram shows the heights, in cm, of a sample of Year 9 girls.
Find for this data:

| | |
|---|---|
| 17 | 0 1 |
| 16 | 2 4 5 7 7 9 |
| 15 | 0 0 2 2 3 4 6 8 8 |
| 14 | 7 8 |

Key:
16 | 2 means 162 cm

**a** the median      **b** the range
**c** the lower quartile      **d** the upper quartile.

**L8** **2** The cumulative frequency graph shows the age distribution of a sample of people at a summer fete.

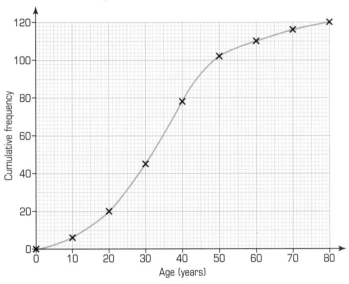

**a** Use the graph to estimate the median and interquartile range of the ages of people at the summer fete.
**b** A similar survey was carried out at a craft fair.
At the craft fair the median age was 47 years and the interquartile range was 32 years.
Compare the age distribution of the people at the summer fete with the people at the craft fair.

**3** A group of people take two reaction time tests, A and B.
Their results are summarised in the cumulative frequency graph.

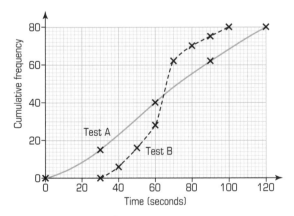

**a** For each test estimate:
   **i** the slowest time      **ii** the range of times
   **iii** the median time      **iv** the interquartile range of times.
**b** Why is test A better to use to discriminate between reaction times?
**c** How many people took longer than 100 seconds to complete test A?

▶ A **scatter graph** is useful for comparing two sets of data with each other.
Plotted points are not joined on a scatter graph.

**KEYWORDS**
Scatter graph          Line of best fit
Correlation

If the points lie roughly in a straight line, there is a relationship or **correlation** between the variables.

Positive correlation          Negative correlation          No correlation

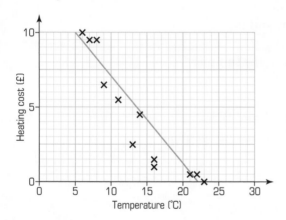

If a graph shows correlation then you can draw a **line of best fit**.

▷ The line of best fit should pass as closely as possible through the points.
▷ There should be about the same number of points above the line as there are below it.
▷ The line does not have to pass through (0, 0).

**example**

The scatter graph shows the daily maximum temperatures and heating costs of a house for the first day of each month over a year.
The diagram also shows a line of best fit for this data.

a Describe the relationship shown by the scatter graph.
b Use the line of best fit to estimate the heating cost when the temperature is 14 °C.
c One day the heating costs were £6.50. Estimate the temperature on that day.

a As the temperature increases the heating costs decrease – negative correlation.
b It will cost about £4.70.
c It must have been about 11 °C.

If the points go upwards there is **positive correlation**.
If they go downwards there is **negative correlation**.

# Exercise D5

**L6**

1   In a competition three games, X, Y and Z, are played.
    The scatter graphs show the scores of all competitors that played all three games.

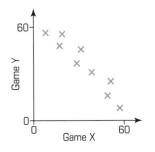 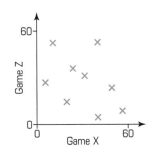

| Perfect negative relationship | Negative relationship | No relationship | Positive relationship | Perfect positive relationship |
|---|---|---|---|---|

Perfect means the points lie exactly on a line.

   a  Choose from the statements above the one that best
      describes the relationship between:
      **i** game X and game Y      **ii** game X and game Z

   b  What can you tell about the relationship between game Y and game Z?
      Sketch a scatter graph showing this relationship. Remember to label the axes.

**L7**

2   Here are some false statements about lines of best fit that can be drawn on scatter graphs.
    Explain why they are false by suggesting an alternative statement.

   a  Lines of best fit must always pass through the origin.
   b  Lines of best fit should join all the points together.
   c  Lines of best fit should always slope upwards.

3   The scatter graph shows the diameter and
    height of a sample of pine trees.
    a  Describe what the scatter graph shows
       about the diameter and height of pine
       trees.
    b  Draw a line of best fit on the graph.
    c  Use the line to estimate the height of a
       pine tree with diameter 20 cm.
    d  Another tree has diameter 10 cm and
       height 14 m.
       Use the graph to explain whether or not you think this is a pine tree.

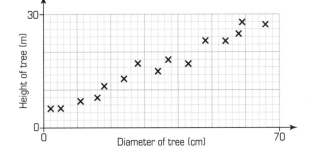

4   The diagram shows the correlation between
    engine capacity (in cm³) and urban fuel
    consumption (in miles per gallon) of a sample
    of cars.
    a  Describe the relationship shown by the scatter
       graph.
    b  Use the line of best fit to estimate the urban
       fuel consumption of a car with engine
       capacity:
       **i** 1500 cm³   **ii** 4000 cm³
    c  Use the line of best fit to estimate the engine
       capacity of a car with urban fuel
       consumption of:
       **i** 15 mpg   **ii** 35 mpg

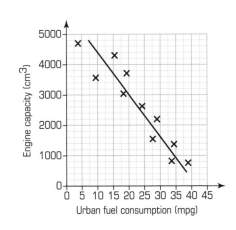

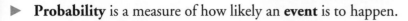

# D6 Probability problems and mutually exclusive events

▶ **Probability** is a measure of how likely an **event** is to happen.

▶ Probabilities are measured on a scale from 0 to 1.
They can be given as fractions, decimals or percentages.

p(A) is a shorthand way of writing 'the probability of event A happening'.

**KEYWORDS**
Probability
Equally likely
Mutually exclusive
Outcome
Expected frequency
Event

When **outcomes** are **equally likely**:

▶ $p(A) = \dfrac{\text{number of ways A can occur}}{\text{total possible number of outcomes}}$

▶ $p(\text{not A}) = 1 - p(A)$

If you know the probability of an event, you can estimate how many times it is likely to occur.

▶ Expected frequency = probability × number of trials

---

**example**

This is a fair six-sided spinner.

a There are only 3 colours, but the probability of white is not $\frac{1}{3}$.
Explain why not.
b Write down the probability that the spinner lands
on **i** blue **ii** not blue.
c The spinner is spun 30 times. How many times would you expect
it to land on white?

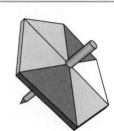

. . . . . . . . . . . . . . . . . . . . . . . . . . . . . . . . . . . . . . . . . . . . . . . . . . . . . . . . . . . . . . . . .

a Only 1 out of 6 sections is white. The spinner is fair so all sections
are equally likely, giving $p(\text{white}) = \frac{1}{6}$.
b **i** $\frac{3}{6} = \frac{1}{2}$   **ii** $1 - \frac{1}{2} = \frac{1}{2}$
c Expected frequency = $\frac{1}{6} \times 30 = 5$ times

---

**example**

There are green and blue counters in a box.
The probability that I choose a green counter is $\frac{1}{5}$.
The first 2 counters that I choose are green.
What is the smallest number of blue counters that could be in
the bag?

. . . . . . . . . . . . . . . . . . . . . . . . . . . . . . . . . . . . . . . . . . . . . . . . . . . . . . . . . . . . . . . . .

Assume the 2 green counters chosen are the only green counters.
Then $p(G) = \frac{1}{5} = \frac{2}{10}$, converting to a fraction with numerator 2.
If 2 out of 10 are green, $10 - 2 = 8$ must be blue.
So the smallest possible number of blue counters is 8.

---

**Mutually exclusive** events cannot occur at the same time.
▶ The sum of all mutually exclusive events is 1.

---

**example**

There are orange (O), lemon (L) and strawberry (S) sweets in a bag.
$p(O) = \frac{5}{12}$   $p(L) = \frac{1}{6}$   $p(S) = \frac{1}{4}$
Are there any other flavour sweets in the bag?
Explain your answer.

. . . . . . . . . . . . . . . . . . . . . . . . . . . . . . . . . . . . . . . . . . . . . . . . . . . . . . . . . . . . . . . . .

$\frac{5}{12} + \frac{1}{6} + \frac{1}{4} = \frac{5}{12} + \frac{2}{12} + \frac{3}{12} = \frac{10}{12} \neq 1$
There must be another flavour sweet in the bag to make the total
probability 1.

---

## Exercise D6

**L6**

**1** There are some counters in a bag. They are either red or yellow. The probability that a red counter is chosen is $\frac{4}{9}$.

  **a** What is the probability of choosing a yellow counter?

One counter is taken out of the bag. It is red.

  **b** What is the smallest number of yellow counters there could be in the bag?

Another counter is taken out of the bag. It is also red.

  **c** Using this extra information, what is the smallest number of yellow counters there could be in the bag?

**2** The probability that Roxy wins a game of noughts and crosses is 0.58. Is she more likely to win or lose the game? Explain how you know.

**3** Chelsea is either early for school, on time or late. The table shows some of the probabilities of each of these occurring on a school day.

  **a** What is the probability that Chelsea is late for school on a school day?

  **b** There are 190 school days in a year. What is the expected number of times that Chelsea will not be late for school during one school year?

| Event | Probability |
|---------|-------------|
| Early | 0.56 |
| On time | 0.33 |
| Late | |

**L7**  **4** I am going to take a marble from a large bag of marbles. The probability that it is green is $\frac{1}{5}$. There are 7 green marbles in the bag. How many marbles are there in the bag that are not green?

**5** In a guessing game the probability that Jack wins is 0.36. Jack plays the game 50 times. How many does he expect to win?

**6** Phoebe plays scrabble with a friend. She wins 24 of the games. She estimates that the probability of winning is 0.3. How many games of scrabble did Phoebe play in total?

**7** Nick plays a game against a computer. The designers of the game say that the computer should win 80% of all games. Nick played the game 400 times and won 84 games. He said the designers of the game were wrong. Do you agree with Nick? Explain your answer.

**L8** **8** I have a large bag of lemon, orange, cherry and strawberry flavoured sweets. I choose one sweet at random. The table shows the probability of each flavour being chosen.

| | Lemon | Orange | Cherry | Strawberry |
|-------------|-------|--------|--------|------------|
| Probability | 0.05 | 0.4 | 0.35 | 0.2 |

  **a** Explain why the number of orange sweets in the bag cannot be 12.
  **b** What is the smallest possible number of each flavour sweet in the bag?
  **c** There are in fact 42 cherry flavoured sweets in the bag. How many sweets in total are there in the bag?

**9** A bag contains green and blue marbles. One marble is chosen from the bag. The probability of choosing a green marble is 0.42.
  **a** Explain why there cannot be 20 marbles in the bag.
  **b** What is the smallest number of marbles there could be in the bag?

In probability you need to list all the possible outcomes systematically.

**KEYWORDS**
Independent
Outcome
Sample space diagram

**example**

Four friends, Ann (A), Ben (B), Carl (C) and Dave (D) have three tickets to a football match.
List the different groups of three that can go to the match.

List the possibilities systematically: ABC, ABD, ACD, BCD.

**example**

Joe has two coins in his pocket, 10p and 2p.
Kath has three coins in her pocket, 20p, 10p and 2p.
They each choose one coin. Each coin is equally likely to be chosen.

a    List the ways in which the coins can be chosen.
b    What is the probability that they both choose coins of the same value?

a

| Joe | 10 | 10 | 10 | 2 | 2 | 2 |
|------|----|----|----|----|----|----|
| Kath | 20 | 10 | 2 | 20 | 10 | 2 |

b    p(both 10p or both 2p) $= \frac{2}{6} = \frac{1}{3}$

You can use a **sample space diagram** to list the outcomes of two events.

**example**

Two 4-sided dice are each numbered 1, 2, 3, 4.
The dice are rolled and there scores are added together.
Draw a sample space diagram to show all possible outcomes.
What is the probability of getting a total of 6?

| + | 1 | 2 | 3 | 4 |
|---|---|---|---|---|
| 1 | 2 | 3 | 4 | 5 |
| 2 | 3 | 4 | 5 | 6 |
| 3 | 4 | 5 | 6 | 7 |
| 4 | 5 | 6 | 7 | 8 |

There are 16 outcomes and 3 totals of 6.
$p(6) = \frac{3}{16}$

▶ Two events are **independent** if the outcome of one event does not affect the outcome of the other event.
▶ If events follow on then you multiply their probabilities.

**example**

At a road junction a cyclist can turn left, right or go straight on.
The probabilities that the cyclist turns left or right are the same.
The probability that the cyclist goes straight on is 0.6.

a    What is the probability that the cyclist turns right?

The cyclist comes to a second road junction and can turn left, right or go straight on.
The probability that the cyclist goes straight on is again 0.6.

b    What is the probability that the cyclist went straight on at both road junctions?

a    $1 - 0.6 = 0.4$      $\frac{1}{2}$ of $0.4 = 0.2$       p(turns right) = 0.2
b    p(straight on and straight on) $= 0.6 \times 0.6 = 0.36$

# Exercise D7

**L6**

**1** Jack has two marbles, red and blue.
Kevin has three marbles, red, yellow and green.
They each choose one of their own marbles.

**a** List the different ways in which the marbles might be chosen.
**b** What is the probability that they choose a marble of the same colour?

**2** The PIN code for a mobile phone contains the four digits 2, 3, 3 and 8.
List the different combinations that the PIN code could be.

**3** Two spinners have three equal sectors.
Each spinner is spun.
The numbers showing are multiplied to get a total.

**a** List all the possible totals.
**b** What is the probability that the total is:
   **i** 2   **ii** 8   **iii** greater than 8?

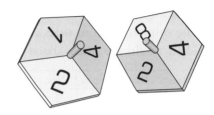

**L7**

**4** A set of cards, with one maths question on each card, are categorised by question type and level of difficulty.
The table shows the probability of selecting a card at random.

|  | Number | Algebra | Shape | Data |
|---|---|---|---|---|
| Easy | 0.24 | 0.2 | 0.15 | 0.16 |
| Difficult | 0.06 | 0.15 | 0.04 | |

One card is taken at random from the set.

**a** What is the probability that it is:

   **i** a shape question     **ii** a difficult question?

There are 80 questions in the set.

**b** How many of these are:
   **i** number questions     **ii** easy questions
   **iii** difficult shape questions?

**5** Three coins are thrown.
**a** List all the different possible outcomes.

Three coins are thrown 400 times.
**b** What is the expected number of times that you would get 1 tail and 2 heads?

**L8**

**6** A company makes mobile phones.
The probability that a phone is defective is 0.05.

**a** Two phones are chosen at random. What is the probability that:
   **i** they are both defective
   **ii** only one of the phones is defective?
**b** The company found four defective phones in a sample they tested.
   How many phones are likely to have been in the sample they tested?

**7** Claire gets maths homework on a Monday.
The probability that she does her maths homework on
Monday evening is $\frac{3}{8}$.
What is the probability that Claire does her maths homework on:

**a** two consecutive Monday evenings
**b** three consecutive Monday evenings?

**8** The probability that the battery in a smoke detector is still working
after 2 years is 0.3. There are 2 smoke detectors in Janie's house.

**a** Calculate the probability that both batteries in the smoke detectors
   will be working after 2 years.
**b** 400 houses each have 2 smoke detectors. In how many of these houses
   will both batteries in the smoke detectors be working after 2 years?

When you do not know the theoretical probability of an event you can estimate it by carrying out an experiment.

▶ **Relative frequency** or experimental probability $= \frac{\text{number of successful trials}}{\text{total number of trials}}$

▶ The more **trials** you carry out the more reliable your estimate of probability will be.

**example**

Five students carried out an experiment to find out whether a spinner is biased.
The spinner has four sides coloured black, blue, grey and white.
Their results are summarised in the table.

| Student | Number of spins | Black | Blue | Grey | White |
|---------|-----------------|-------|------|------|-------|
| A | 40 | 8 | 16 | 10 | 6 |
| B | 50 | 12 | 14 | 11 | 13 |
| C | 100 | 27 | 29 | 25 | 19 |
| D | 10 | 2 | 4 | 2 | 2 |
| E | 50 | 9 | 14 | 13 | 14 |

**a** Which student's data should give the best estimates for experimental probability? Explain your answer.

They collected all their results together in the following table.

| Colour | Black | Blue | Grey | White |
|--------|-------|------|------|-------|
| Frequency | 58 | 77 | 61 | 54 |

**b** Write down whether you think the spinner is biased. Explain your answer.

**c** What is the probability that the spinner lands on
  **i** blue     **ii** white?

........................................................................................................

**a** Student C because there were many more spins.
**b** If the spinner is fair, each colour should have come up about the same number of times. Blue came up a lot more than any other colour, so the spinner may be biased.
**c** **i** $\frac{77}{250}$     **ii** $\frac{54}{250}$

You can draw a graph to show how the probability changes.

**example**

Faye planted crocuses that had purple or white flowers.
She did not know how many of each colour there were.
Faye noted the colour of each flower as they opened.
She calculated the fraction of purple flowers each time.
Faye drew a graph to show how the probability changed.

**a** Use the graph to find the colours of the first three flowers.
**b** Estimate the percentage of flowers that are purple.

........................................................................................

**a** First flower was white (as probability of purple is zero), second flower was purple (as probability of purple is now $\frac{1}{2}$), third flower was white (as probability of purple dropped to $\frac{1}{3}$).
**b** The probability of purple tends towards 0.3, as a percentage this is 30%.

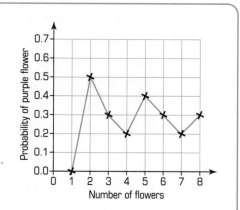

## Exercise D8

**1** Four students carried out an experiment to see if a coin was biased.
The data they collected is shown in this table.

| | Lexie | Chloe | Rachel | Louis |
|---|---|---|---|---|
| Heads | 29 | 120 | 38 | 246 |
| Tails | 21 | 120 | 42 | 254 |

  **a** Whose data is likely to give the most reliable answer to whether or not the coin is biased? Explain your answer.

They collected their data together in the this table.

| Heads | 433 |
|---|---|
| Tails | 437 |

  **b** Do you think the coin is biased? Explain your answer.
  **c** Use the data to work out the probability of the coin showing tails.

**2** A bag contains a large number of seeds that are purple or white.
Richard and Pat each select 100 seeds at random.
Each seed is returned to the bag before another is selected.

These are their results.

| | Purple | White |
|---|---|---|
| Richard | 51 | 49 |
| Pat | 46 | 54 |

  **a** Write down the relative frequencies of purple and white seeds for Richard and Pat.
  **b** Work out the relative frequency of purple and white seeds for their combined results.
  **c** Which relative frequencies are likely to be the most accurate estimate of the probability that a selected seed is purple or white?
  **d** If there are 20 000 seeds in the bag estimate the number of purple seeds.

**3** Lauren carries out an experiment with a group of 10 coins.
She drops the coins and notes how many of them show heads.
She repeats this experiment 12 times.

> **Number of coins that show heads**
> 3   6   5   7   6   5   7   4   5   2   3   4

  **a** Use Lauren's data to work out the probability that a single coin when dropped will show heads. Show your working.

Lauren continues the experiment until she has dropped the group of 10 coins 40 times.

  **b** About how many of the coins in total would you expect to show heads?

**4** A chef records the number of eggs that contain double yolks in each box he uses.
(Each box contains 6 eggs.)

| Number of double yolks | 0 | 1 | 2 | 3 | 4 | 5 | 6 |
|---|---|---|---|---|---|---|---|
| Number of boxes | 4 | 4 | 5 | 8 | 7 | 3 | 1 |

  **a** Work out the probability that the next box of 6 eggs the chef opens will contain:
    **i** no eggs with double yolks    **ii** 2 or 3 eggs with double yolks.
  **b** What is the probability that the next two boxes that are opened will each contain 6 eggs with double yolks?

**5** Jenny had a coin that she suspected was biased.
She threw the coin ten times and calculated the probability of getting a head after each throw.
The graph shows the results for the first ten throws.

  **a** For each of the first three throws write down whether Jenny got heads or tails.
  **b** What percentage of the throws showed heads?
  **c** Estimate the probability that Jenny will get a head on the next throw of the coin.
  **d** Jenny said the coin was biased. Do you agree with Jenny? Explain your answer.

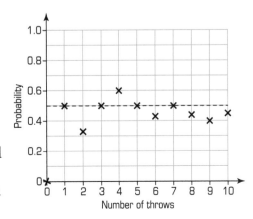

**L6**

1  The scatter diagram shows the heights and masses of some horses.
The scatter diagram also shows a line of best fit.

**D5**

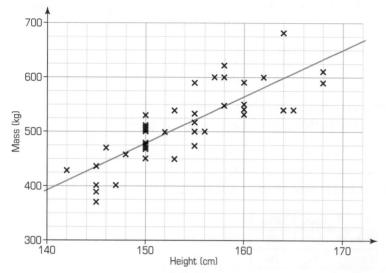

Height (cm)

Mass (kg)

a  What does the scatter diagram show about the **relationship** between the height and mass of horses?

b  The **height** of a horse is **163 cm**.
Use the line of best fit to estimate the mass of the horse.

c  A different horse has a **mass of 625 kg**.
Use the line of best fit to estimate the height of the horse.

d  A teacher asks his class to investigate this statement:

"The length of the **back leg** of a horse is **always less than** the length of the **front leg** of a horse."

What might a scatter graph look like if the statement is correct?

2  I have two bags of counters.

**Bag A** contains **12 red** counters and **18 yellow** counters.
**Bag B** contains **10 red** counters and **16 yellow** counters.

I am going to take one counter at random from either bag A or bag B.

I want to get a **red** counter. Which bag should I choose?
Show working to explain your answer.

**D6**

**L7**

3  Owls eat small mammals.
They regurgitate the bones and fur in balls called pellets.
The table shows the contents of **62** pellets from long-eared owls.

**D3**

| Number of mammals found in the pellet | 1 | 2 | 3 | 4 | 5 | 6 |
|---|---|---|---|---|---|---|
| Frequency | 9 | 17 | 24 | 6 | 5 | 1 |

a  Show that the **total** number of mammals found is **170**.

b  Calculate the **mean** number of mammals found in each pellet.
Show your working and give your answer correct to 1 decimal place.

c  There are about **10 000** long-eared owls in Britain.
On average, a long-eared owl regurgitates **1.4** pellets per day.
Altogether, how many **mammals** do the 10 000 long-eared owls eat in **one day**?
Show your working and give your answer to the nearest thousand.

**L7**

**4** A headteacher wants to choose a pupil from year 7, 8 or 9 to appear on television.
The headteacher gives each pupil **one** ticket.
Then she will select the winning ticket at random.
The table shows information about the ticket used.

**D7**

| | Colour of the ticket | Numbers used |
|---|---|---|
| Year 7 | red | 1 to 80 |
| Year 8 | blue | 1 to 75 |
| Year 9 | yellow | 1 to 90 |

**a** What is the probability that the winning ticket will be **blue**?

**b** What is the probability that the winning ticket will show number **39**?

**c** The headteacher selects the winning ticket at random.
She says:

'The winning ticket number is 39'.

What is the probability that this winning ticket is blue?

**L8**

**5** A company makes computer disks.
It tested a random sample of disks from a large batch.
The company calculated the probability of any disk being defective as 0.025.
Glenda buys two disks.

**D7**

**a** Calculate the probability that **both** disks are defective.

**b** Calculate the probability that **only one** of the disks is defective.

**c** The company found 3 defective disks in the sample they tested.
How many disks were likely to have been tested?

**6** A girl plays the same computer game lots of times.
The computer scores each game using **1 for win, 0 for lose**.
After each game, the computer calculates her **overall mean score**.
The graph shows the results for the first **20 games**.

**D8**

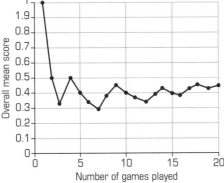

**a** For each of **the first 3** games, write whether the girl won or lost.

**b** What percentage of the 20 games did the girl win?

The graph below shows the girl's results for the first 100 games.

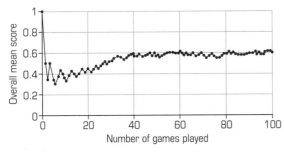

**c** She is going to play the game again.
Estimate the probability that she will win.

**d** Suppose for the 101st to 120th games, the girl were to **lose each game**.
What would the graph look like up to the 120th game?
Show your answer on a sketch graph.

▶ This test is 1 hour long.
▶ You **must not** use a calculator for any question in this test.
▶ You will need: pen, pencil, rubber, ruler, paper and graph paper.

**1 a** A function maps the number $n$ to the number $n + 3$.
Copy the table and complete the missing values.

$$n \rightarrow n + 3$$
$$5 \rightarrow \ldots$$
$$\ldots \rightarrow 28$$

*(1 mark)*

**b** A different function maps the number $n$ to $4n$.
Copy the table and complete the missing values.

$$n \rightarrow 4n$$
$$5 \rightarrow \ldots$$
$$\ldots \rightarrow 28$$

*(1 mark)*

**c** Many different functions can map the number 8 to the number 2.
Copy and complete the tables by wring two different functions.

$$n \rightarrow \ldots \qquad n \rightarrow \ldots$$
$$8 \rightarrow 2 \qquad 8 \rightarrow 2$$

*(2 marks)*

**2** You can make three different cuboids using 27 cubes.

| | | Dimensions | | |
|---|---|---|---|---|
| Cuboid A | | 1 | 1 | 27 |
| Cuboid B | | 1 | 3 | 9 |
| Cuboid C | | 3 | 3 | 3 |

**a** Which of the cuboids has the smallest surface area or do they all have the same surface area?
Explain how you know. *(1 mark)*

**b** Which cuboid has the largest volume or do they all have the same volume?
Explain how you know. *(1 mark)*

**c** How many of cuboid B would you need to make a cube with dimensions $9 \times 9 \times 9$? *(1 mark)*

**d** You can make three different cuboids with 18 cubes.
What are the dimensions of each cuboid? *(3 marks)*

**3** These shapes are drawn on square grids

**Shape A**

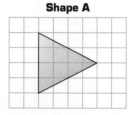

**Shape B**

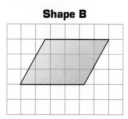

**Shape C**

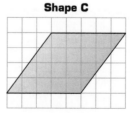

**a** What type of triangle is shape A? *(1 mark)*
**b** Is shape B a parallelogram? Explain how you know. *(1 mark)*
**c** Is shape C a square? Explain how you know. *(1 mark)*

4  Copy the table and write in the missing numbers
   The first row is done for you.

| 1st number | 2nd number | Sum of 1st and 2nd numbers | Product of 1st and 2nd numbers |
|---|---|---|---|
| 9 | 2 | 11 | 18 |
| 7 | ⁻3 |  |  |
| 5 |  | ⁻1 |  |

*(1 mark)*

*(1 mark)*

5  **a** Calculate $\frac{8}{9} \times \frac{3}{4}$. Show your working.
      Write your answer as a fraction in its simplest form.          *(2 marks)*
   **b** In a school sixth form, two fifths of the students are male.
      One sixth of these males wear glasses.
      What fraction of the sixth form are males that wear glasses?          *(1 mark)*

6  **a** Rearrange these equations    **i**    $x + 5 = y$          *(1 mark)*
      to the form $x = ...$        **ii**   $3x = y$          *(1 mark)*
                           **iii**  $x - 2 = 8y$          *(1 mark)*
   **b** Rearrange this equation to make $x$ the subject.    $3(4 + x) = y$          *(2 marks)*

7  Two people, Joshua and Reuben, travel from A to B
   along different routes.
   Their journeys take the same amount of time.
   Joshua travels at an average speed of 40 km/h.
   What is Reuben's average speed?          *(2 marks)*

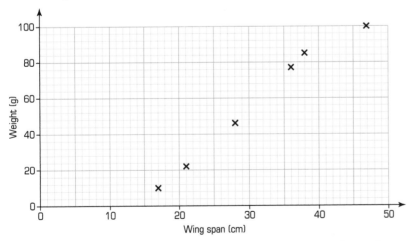

8  **a** Which of the following expressions is the same as $x^2 - 7x + 6$?          *(1 mark)*

      $(x + 1)(x + 6)$

                           $(x + 1)(x - 6)$

            $(x + 6)(x + 1)$                    $(x - 1)(x - 6)$

   **b** Multiply out the expression $(x + 3)(x + 7)$.
      Write your answer as simply as possible.          *(3 marks)*

9  The scatter graph shows the average wingspan and the average weight of
   different species of birds.

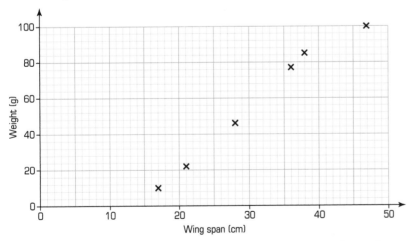

   **a** What does the scatter graph tell you about the type of correlation
      between average wingspan and weight of this sample of birds?          *(1 mark)*
   **b** Draw a line of best fit on the scatter graph.          *(1 mark)*
   **c** If the wingspan increased by 10 cm, by how much would you
      expect the weight to increase?          *(1 mark)*
   **d** A bird has a wingspan of 47 cm and weight of 32 g.
      Is it likely to be one of this species of bird? Explain your answer.          *(1 mark)*

**10** I have two fair four-sided dice.
One is numbered 2, 3, 5 and 7.
The other is numbered 1, 2, 4 and 8.
I throw both dice and multiply the scores.
What is the probability that the total is even?
Show your working to explain your answer.

*(2 marks)*

**11** The table shows a recipe for fruit punch.

| Juice | Amount |
|---|---|
| Orange | $\frac{3}{8}$ litre |
| Lime | $\frac{1}{8}$ litre |
| Lemonade | $\frac{1}{2}$ litre |
| Total | 1 litre |

I want to make $1\frac{1}{2}$ litres of the same drink.
How much of each type of juice should I use?

*(3 marks)*

**12** Think about rectangles with

> a perimeter of 16 cm
> each side is a whole number of centimetres

Prove that there are only four of these rectangles.

*(3 marks)*

**13** The table shows data about the lengths of some rivers in metres.

| River | Length, m |
|---|---|
| Nile | $6.7 \times 10^7$ |
| Amazon | $6.4 \times 10^7$ |
| Danube | $2.8 \times 10^7$ |
| Thames | $3.4 \times 10^6$ |

  **a** Which of the rivers listed in the table is the shortest? *(1 mark)*
  **b** How much longer is the river Nile than the river Amazon?
   Show your working and write your answer in standard form. *(2 marks)*

**14 a** Look at these equations.   $40 = 5 \times 2^a$   $52 = 13 \times 2^b$
   What are the values of $a$ and $b$? *(1 mark)*
  **b** $40 \times 52 = 5 \times 13 \times 2^c$.
   What is the value of $c$? *(1 mark)*

**15** The chart shows the original population of some species of whale in the year that
they became protected and their current estimated population.

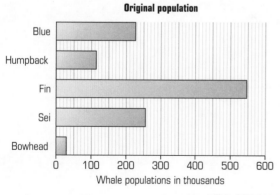
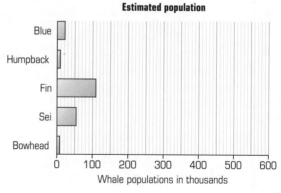

  **a** Use the information in the chart to decide if the statement below is true or false
   or there is not enough information to tell.

   'The estimated percentage of Sei whales is about the same as the percentage of Sei
   whales in the original population.'
   Explain your answer. *(1 mark)*
  **b** Approximately what is the percentage decrease in the number of Blue whales? *(1 mark)*
  **c** Approximately what is the percentage decrease in the number of Bowhead whales? *(1 mark)*
  **d** Write a sentence about the change in whale population. *(1 mark)*

**16** A pupil recorded the arm span of all the girls in her school year.
She summarised her results and then drew this box plot.

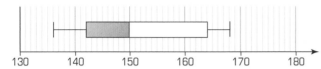

The pupil compared the arm span of the boys in the same year group as the girls:
▷ the boy with the greatest arm span had the same arm span as the girl with the greatest arm span
▷ the range of boys' arm span was less than the range of girls' arm span
▷ the interquartile range of boy's arm span was greater than the interquartile range of the girls' arm span
▷ the boys and girls had the same median arm span.
**a** Draw what the box plot for the boys could look like.                    (*2 marks*)

In the same year group at another school there were 100 girls.
The cumulative frequency diagram shows information about their arm span.

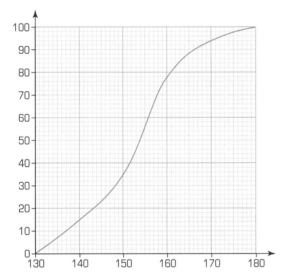

**b** Compare the arm span of the girls in the two different schools.          (*3 marks*)

**17** Match each graph to the correct equation.

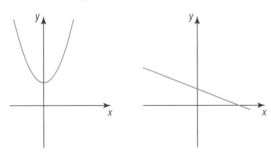   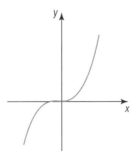   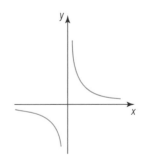

Choose from the equations below.

P: $y = 2 - x$     Q: $y = \frac{2}{x}$     R: $y = x^2 + 2$     S: $y = 2x^3$          (*2 marks*)

**18** I start with any three consecutive integers.
I multiply the three integers together.
Prove that the total must be divisible by 3.                    (*3 marks*)

▶ This test is 1 hour long.

▶ You may use a calculator for any question in this test.

▶ You will need: pen, pencil, rubber, ruler, compasses, calculator, paper and graph paper.

**1** The triangle and the rectangle below have the same area.

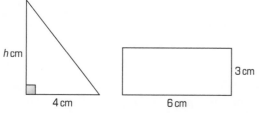

Work out the value of *h*. Show your working.     *(2 marks)*

**2** What percentage of £9840 is £3460?

Show your working and give your answer to the nearest whole number.     *(2 marks)*

**3** The graph shows a straight line.

   **a** Write down the coordinates of three
       points that lie on the line.     *(1 mark)*

   **b** Write an equation of the straight line.     *(1 mark)*

   **c** On the graph, draw the straight line
       that has the equation $x + y = 3$.     *(1 mark)*

**4** There are 18 questions in a quiz.

A correct answer scores 4 points. An incorrect answer loses 3 points.

A question not answered scores nothing. It is possible to have a negative total.

   **a** What are the maximum and minimum points that you could score on the quiz?     *(1 mark)*

   **b** A pupil answers 7 of the questions. 3 are correct.
       Explain why this pupil's total score is zero.     *(1 mark)*

   **c** Write down three different ways in which a pupil could have a total score of 12 points.     *(3 marks)*

**5**  **a** The cross-section of a cylindrical tube is a circle.
       The radius of this circle is 4 cm.
       What is the area of this circle?     *(1 mark)*

   **b** I can fill this tube with 460 cm$^3$ of water.
       What is the height of the tube? Give your answer to the nearest whole number.     *(2 marks)*

**6**  **a** Use the formula $y = \dfrac{x+5}{2x}$ to find the value of *y* when $x = 4$.     *(2 marks)*

   **b** Use the same formula to find the value of *x* when $y = \frac{2}{3}$.     *(2 marks)*

**7**  **a** A teacher asked a class of pupils what mobile phone
       network they used.
       The pie chart shows the results.

       5 pupils answered T-mobile.

       How many pupils answered Vodafone?     *(1 mark)*

   **b** In another class there were 30 pupils.
       The teacher asked this class what mobile phone
       network they used.
       4 pupils answered Orange.
       On a pie chart what would be the angle for the sector Orange?     *(2 marks)*

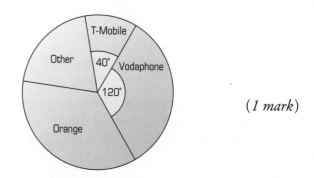

**8** One shade of brown paint is made by mixing red, yellow and blue
paints in the ratio $4:5:3$.

   **a** In one pot of paint the amount of blue paint used is 150 ml.
How much of the other two paint colours are used?                    *(1 mark)*

   **b** In a tester paint pot 10 ml of red paint is used.
How much of the other two paint colours are used?                    *(2 marks)*

**9** Altogether I have 12 bags of marbles.
The mean number of marbles in the bags is 24.
There are 3 bags with 22 marbles, 5 bags with 23 marbles, 1 bag with 24 marbles
and 2 bags with 27 marbles.
How many marbles are there in the twelfth bag?                    *(2 marks)*

**10** The diagram shows a regualar octagon with 8 isosceles triangles.
It is constructed using straight lines.

   **a** Without measuring explain why angle $x$ must be 135°.                    *(1 mark)*

   **b** Calculate the size of angle $y$.
Show your working.                    *(1 mark)*

   **c** On the diagram use compasses and a straight edge to
construct the perpendicular bisector of P and Q.
Leave in your construction lines.                    *(2 marks)*

**11** Some numbers are smaller than their cubes.

For example $2 < 2^3$

   **a** Which numbers are equal to their cubes?                    *(2 marks)*

   **b** Some numbers are bigger than their cubes.
Describe this set of numbers.                    *(2 marks)*

**12** Is it possible to have a triangle with the angles and lengths shown below?
For each triangle, show calculations to support your answer.

   **a**

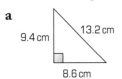

                                                         *(2 marks)*

   **b**

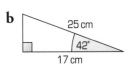

                                                         *(2 marks)*

**13** Natalie uses a rowing machine to keep fit.
The simplified distance–time graph shows how she
used the machine during one exercise session.
Use the graph to answer these questions.

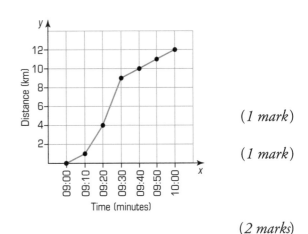

   **a** Between 09:10 and 09:20 of the exercise session
what was Natalie's speed in kilometres per hour?                    *(1 mark)*

   **b** Throughout the exercise session, for how many
minutes did she travel at this speed?                    *(1 mark)*

   **c** For the first 10 minutes her speed was slower
than the second 10 minutes of the session.
By how many kilometres per hour was her
speed slower?                    *(2 marks)*

**14** Look at these expressions.

$8x + 7$        $4x - 9$

   **a** What value of $x$ makes the two expressions equal?
Show your working.                                                    *(2 marks)*
   **b** What value of $x$ makes the second expression three times as great
as the first expression?
Show your working.                                                    *(2 marks)*

**15** Each pattern below shows a rectangular shape, made from squares,
that is three squares high.
The corners of the shape are shaded.
All squares in the middle row are shaded.

Imagine one of these patterns that has $n$ squares in each row.
Write an expression for the fraction of the pattern that is shaded.     *(2 marks)*

**16** People were asked if they were considering changing their car in the
next six months.
42% of the people asked said yes.
Of these, 78% said they were considering buying a small car.
What percentage of the people asked said they were considering buying
a small car?                                                          *(1 mark)*

**17** Solve this equation.

$$\frac{7(3x - 1)}{5x} = 4$$

Show your working.                                                     *(2 marks)*

**18** Calculate the length of the diagonal of a square of length 9 cm.          *(2 marks)*

**19** A student has two shapes of tiles.
One is a pentagon and one is a square.
The side length of each tile is the same.
The student says the tiles will fit like this.
Show calculations to prove that the student is wrong.                  *(3 marks)*

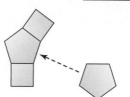

**20** The diagram shows a rectangle inside a triangle.

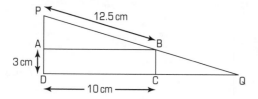

PBQ is a straight line.
The rectangle has side lengths 3 cm by 10 cm as shown.
PB = 12.5 cm.
Show that the length BQ = 5 cm.                                        *(3 marks)*

# Answers

## Exercise N1

**1 a** 29.5%  **b** 23 128   **2 a** 50.5%  **b** 71

**3** Yes. The distance was measured to the nearest cm, so it could have been up to 0.5 cm longer.

**4** 16.65 and 16.75   **5** 169.5 and 170.5   **6** 6350 kg   **7** $39 \times 10^6$   **8** $4.14 \times 10^6$ mm   **9** $2.1 \times 10^{-1}$

**10** $8.65 \times 10^5$ miles

**11** About 3.7 times   **12 a** $5 \times 10^{-5}$  **b** $5 \times 10^{-6}$  **c** $5.5 \times 10^{-5}$   **13** 6   **14** $1.426 \times 10^{22}$   **15** $1.5125 \times 10^{16}$

## Exercise N2

**1** 216   **2** 90 000   **3** 9   **4** 100   **5** 4   **6 a** $1^7$  **b** $2^5$  **c** $3^4$ and $9^2$

**7** 6 cm and 2 cm, 3 cm and 4 cm, 12 cm and 1 cm   **8 a i** $^+5$  **ii** $^-2$  **b** $^-3 - {}^+9 = {}^-12$  **c** $^-3 - {}^-6 = {}^+3$

**9** $2 \times 2 \times 2 \times 3 \times 3$   **10** 12   **11** 6   **12 a** 9  **b** 7  **c** 6   **13** $k = 6$   **14** $2 \times 2 \times 2 \times 3 \times 5$   **15** 9

**16** 128   **17** 1 000 000 000 000   **18** $x = 2, y = 4$   **19** 729   **20 a** $0.4n$  **b** $\sqrt[3]{n}, \frac{1}{n}, n^3$  **c** $0.4n, n^3$  **d** $\frac{n}{0.4}, n^3$

**21 a** Because $6^2 \times 6^3 = 6^5 = 7776$  **b** 1296 ($6^4$)

## Exercise N3

**1** 5   **2 a** $\frac{9}{14}$  **b** $\frac{14}{33}$   **3** 49% ($\frac{4}{9} = 44.4\% < 49\%$)   **4** 27% ($\frac{2}{7} = 28.6\% > 27\%$)   **5 a** $15\frac{1}{2}$  **b** $4\frac{3}{7}$

**6 a** $\frac{1}{5}, \frac{2}{7}$  **b** $\frac{1}{2} + \frac{1}{5} + \frac{3}{10}$  **c** $\frac{2}{7}$   **7 a** 0.002 and 0.1  **b** 0.002 and 5  **c** $\frac{4}{0.4}$

**8 a i** $\frac{13}{40}$  **ii** $\frac{3}{10}$  **b i** $\frac{1}{2} + \frac{1}{3}$  **ii** $\frac{1}{3} - \frac{1}{5}$ or $\frac{1}{10} + \frac{1}{30}$  **c** $\frac{7}{12}$  **d** $\frac{3}{1} + \frac{1}{5}$  **e** $\frac{1}{4} + \frac{1}{7}$

**9 a** $0.01 \times 0.2 = 0.002$  **b** $4 \div 0.2 = 20$, or $0.2 \div 0.01 = 20$.   **10 a** $\frac{9}{56}$  **b** $1\frac{2}{5}$  **c** $6\frac{7}{8}$   **11 a** $\frac{7}{16}$  **b** $\frac{16}{27}$  **c** $3\frac{3}{4}$

**12 a** $1\frac{7}{20}$  **b** $\frac{2}{3}$  **c** $\frac{5}{6}$   **13 a** $3\frac{3}{4}$  **b** $3\frac{3}{10}$

## Exercise N4

**1 a** £12 : £48  **b** £67.5 : £40.5   **2** 78.125 calories   **3 a** 5 : 4  **b** 6 : 5  **c** 6 (Joshua) and 3 (Reuben)

**4 a** 52%  **b** 48.6%  **c** tub   **5** 52   **6 a** 1.53  **b** 0.79   **7 a** 48.72  **b** 35.7

**8** Option ii) involves paying less, by £9.94

**9 a** £32.81  **b** 7 days  **c** Because 10% of each new value is subtracted, not 10% of the original value.

**10** 69   **11 a** $42 \times 1.07$  **b** $42 \times 0.07$: what is 7% of 42?
$42 \times 0.7$: what is 70% of 42?
$42 \times 1.7$: increase 42 by 70%

**12** 0.93   **13** 14.49%   **14** £32

## Exercise N5

**1** 99 mm   **2 a** 4.8  **b** 23.4   **3** 10.78 cm   **4** 60   **5** 5.3   **6** 260   **7** 70

**8 a** 21 402  **b** 2.1402  **c** 2140.2  **d** 580   **9** 577.15   **10** £66.74   **11** 480   **12** 320

**13 a** $0.5^3$ You are multiplying by a small number.
**b** $\frac{1}{0.5^2}$ You are dividing by a small number.

**14** c   **15** $0.05^2, 0.05, \sqrt{0.05}, \frac{1}{0.05}$   **16** A is true   **17** 125%

## Exercise N6

**1 a** 61  **b** 21   **2** 3.22322   **3** 0.0001   **4 a** $875.8 \div 4 = 218.95$  **b** $762.1 \div 5 = 152.41$  **c** $2800 \div 8 = 350$

**5** Because $\frac{3}{4}$ is smaller than 1, it will go into it more than once. $1\frac{1}{3}$   **6 a** 7.1  **b** $4\frac{2}{5}$

**7 a** 10  **b** 0.001  **c** 0.005, 0.1  **d i** $0.02 \times 0.005 = 1 \times 10^{-4}$  **ii** $0.005 \div 10 = 0.0005$  **e** $10 + 2.5 = 12.5$

**f** $10 \times 0.02 \times 0.005$   **8 a** 4  **b** 6   **9 a** 5  **b** 6   **10** $5 \times 10^3 = 5000, 2 \times 10^5 = 200\,000, 5000 \times 40 = 200\,000$

**11 a** 0.02  **b** 20   **12** 4   **13** 8.38   **14** The power is smaller

**15 i** 0.368p per gram  **ii** 0.345p per gram  so **ii** is better value for the customer

## Revision R1

**1 a** $^+9$  **b** $^-8$   **2 a** $\frac{7}{16}$  **b** £60   **3 a** $\frac{7}{10}$  **b** $\frac{1}{5}$

**4 a** Yes. It could have been 0.5 cm more.  **b** 14.55 and 14.65

**5 a** 8  **b** 16  **c** 6  **d** estimate between 28 and 34

**6 a** $k = 3, m = 6$  **b** 16 384

**7 a** $0.05 \times 0.1 = 0.005$  **b** $10 \div 0.1 = 100$

**8 a** 48% (2 sf)  **b** 1 : 5.8  **c** $\frac{108}{480} = 0.44$ (2 dp)

**9 a** $3.1 \times 10^5$  **b** $9.2 \times 10^5$  **c** 8.3 km

**10 a** $0.8n$  **b** $n^2, \sqrt{n}, \frac{1}{n}$  **c** $\sqrt{n}, 0.8n, \frac{1}{n}$  **d** $0.8n, n^2$

## Exercise N7

**1** 2.3 and 2.4   **2** 2.1 and 2.2, $^-3.1$ and $^-3.2$   **3 a** 3.938 461 538  **b** 3.9 litres   **4** 8.6 days

**5 a i** 124 987.6943  **ii** 120 000  **b i** 9251.296 643  **ii** 9300  **c i** 1.193 125  **ii** 1.2

**6** Approximately 109 times   **7** It is negative and you can't have a negative volume.

**8 a i** $1.94 \times 10^5$ mps  **ii** $2.08 \times 10^{-1}$ mps  **b** 930 000 times faster

## Exercise A1

**1 a** $7a - 9$ **b** $b + 11$ **c** $7c$ **2 a** $2n + 32$ **b** $64 + n$ **3** $14n$ **4 a** $2x + 4$ **b** $13x - 2$ **c** $17x - 26$
**5** $\frac{b-a}{ab}$ **6 a** $6m + 4n$ **b** Top: $6m + n$; middle: $3m + 2n$; bottom: $2m$. **7 a** $6ab^4$ **b** $\frac{5a^2b}{c}$
**8 a** $3(x - 2)$ **b** $6x(x + 3)$ **9 a** $a^7$ **b** $a^3b^2$ **c** $12a^4b^5$ **d** $a^9$ **e** $3a^4$ **10** $(x + 5)^2 = x^2 + 10x + 25 \neq x^2 + 25$
**11 a** $x^2 + 8x + 15$ **b** $x^2 + x - 12$ **c** $x^2 + 8x + 16$ **d** $x^2 - 6x + 9$ **12** $(x - y)$ **13** $\frac{1}{4}y(x^3 + y)$
**14 a** $x^2 + 12x + 35$ **b** $x^2 + 4x - 12$ **c** $x^2 - 4x + 3$ **15** $(x + 3)^2 - (x + 2)^2 = (x^2 + 6x + 9) - (x^2 + 4x + 4)$
$\qquad\qquad\qquad\qquad\qquad\qquad\qquad\qquad = x^2 - x^2 + 6x - 4x + 9 - 4 = 2x + 5$

## Exercise A2

**1 a** £163 **b** 91 miles **2 a** $x = 12$ **b** $y = 17.5$ **3** 15.4 **4** $x = \frac{1}{2}y - 7$ **5** $x = \frac{1}{3}(6a - y)$
**6 a** 2.061552813 **b** 2.06 and $^-$2.06 **7 a** $x = 5$ **b** $x = 4$ **8 a** $x = {}^-2$ **b** $x = 8$
**9 a** $x = 9.6$ **b** $y = 0.5$ **10 a** $n^3, \sqrt{n}, \frac{1}{n}$ **b** $0.2n, n^3$ **c** $n^3, \frac{n}{0.2}$ **d** $\frac{n}{0.2}$ **11** $k = {}^-0.013$
**12** $x(x + 6) = (x + 1)(x + 4)$
$\quad x^2 + 6x = x^2 + 5x + 4$
$\qquad\qquad x = 4$

## Exercise A3

**1** $x = \frac{3}{2}$ **2** $2x + 5 = 4x - 2$, $x = 3.5$ **3** $m = 4$ **4 a** 9 and $^-$2 **b** 2 and $^-$9 **c** $^-$8 and $^-$3 **5** A is true
**6** Both 25 and $x^2$ are square numbers and square numbers multiplied together always give a square number.
**7** $2x - 5 = 17$: one value of $x$.
$\quad 4(x + 2) = 4x + 8$: all values of $x$.
$\quad x - 1 = x + 1$: no value of $x$.
$\quad x - 7 = 7 - x$: one value of $x$.
$\quad x^2 = 16$: two values of $x$.
**8** $x = 3$
**9** $y = 9.5$, $x = 14.5$
**10 a** e.g. if $x = 1$, $x^2 = 1$ and so $49 + x^2 = 50$, which is not a square number
**b** Two square numbers multiplied together always give another square number.

## Exercise A4

**1 a** C **b** The equation is linear and has an integer solution
**2 a**

| $x$ | 2 | 3 |
|---|---|---|
| $y$ | 5 | 11 |

**b** 0.6 and 0.7, $^-$1.6 and $^-$1.7 **3** 1.9 **4 a** 34 km/h **b** 43 km/h
**5 a** 1.8 and 1.9 **b** 1.84 and 1.85 **6** 23 and 24

## Exercise A5

**1 a i** $b = 1$, $w = 20$ **ii** $b = 1$, $w = 36$ **iii** $b = 1$, $w = 4(P - 1)$ **b** $T = 4P - 3$
**2 a i** 23, 27 **ii** $4n + 3$ **b i** 39, 47 **ii** $8n - 1$ **c i** 25, 36 **ii** $n^2$ **d i** 26, 37 **ii** $n^2 + 1$
**3** $\frac{n}{3n - 1}$ **4** $\frac{3}{5}, \frac{5}{7}, \frac{7}{9}$ **5 a** $^-$1 and 9 **b)** 2 **6** $n^2 = (n - 1)^2 + 2n - 1$ **7** $P = BN$
**8 a**

| Men | 1 | 2 | 4 | 5 | 10 |
|---|---|---|---|---|---|
| Days | 60 | 30 | 15 | 12 | 6 |

**b** $H = MD$

## Revision R2

**1 i** $4d + 3$ **ii** $4m$ **2 a i** 23 **ii** 19.75 **b i** 5.81 (2 dp) **ii** 0.98 (2 dp)
**3** For example, when $t = 2$ and $w = 4$, $\frac{1}{2} + \frac{1}{4} \neq \frac{2}{6}$ **4 a** $e = -f + \frac{p}{2}$ **b** $d = c - 2r$
**5 a i** 1500 **ii** 20 **b** $0.6d$ or $\frac{3d}{5}$ **c i** $9x - 14$ **ii** $x^2 + 5x + 6$ **iii** $x^2 + 3x - 4$ **iv** $x^2 - 4x + 4$
**6** $3x + 7 = 8$: correct for one value of $x$
$\quad 3(x + 1) = 3x + 3$: correct for all value of $x$
$\quad x + 3 = x - 3$: correct for no values of $x$
$\quad 5 + x = 5 - x$: correct for one value of $x$.
$\quad x^2 = 9$: correct for two values of $x$
**7 a i** False **ii** False **iii** True **iv** True **v** True **vi** True **b** It takes a long time and is inefficient.
**8 a** $y$ values: $^-$3, $^-$5, $^-$5 **b** $x = 1.8$
**9 a** $(y + 3)^2 = (y + 3)(y + 3) = y^2 + 6y + 9$ **b i** $y^2 + 7y + 10$ **ii** $y^2 - 12y + 36$ **iii** $6y^2 - y - 40$

## Exercise A6

**1 a**

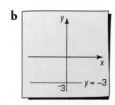

**b**

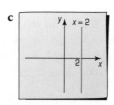

**c**

**2** Yes. $3 \times 20 = 60$ **3** No. $(2 \times 2) + 1 \neq 7$ **4 a** $y = 2$ **b** $x + y = 5$

**5 a**

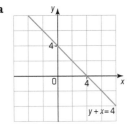

**b**

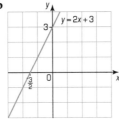

**6 a** D and E  **b** E  **c** B  **d** A and C

**7** e.g $\frac{(2-1)}{(4-0)} = \frac{1}{4}$, generally $\frac{y-y_1}{x-x_1}$ = gradient

**8 a i** $x = 3$  **ii** $y = 3$  **b** A and F  **c** $y = 5$, $x = 4$

**9 a** $\frac{5-1}{0-2} = \frac{4}{-2} = {}^-2$  **b** $y = -2x + 5$  **c** $y = -2x +$ any other number

### Exercise A7

**1 a**

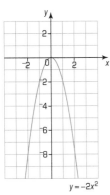

**b** $y = x^2$

**2 a i** $^+2$ and $^-2$  **ii** $^-4$  **b** $y = x^2 - 3$  **c i** 4  **ii** $y = -x^2 + 4$

**3 a i** $(3, 0)$ and $(^-3, 0)$  **ii** $(0, 9)$  **b** $y = x^2 + 1$

**4** $y \leqslant x^2 - 3$, $y \leqslant 0$

### Exercise A8

**1 a** 4 and 5  **b** $^-4$ and 5  **2 a**

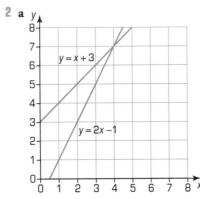

**b** $x = 4$, $y = 7$

**3 a** $x = 1.5$, $y = 4$  **b** $x = \frac{11}{5}$, $y = \frac{9}{5}$  **c** $x = 3.15$, $y = 1.45$

**4** £5.40

**5** 2, 3, 4, 5, 6, 7

**6 a**

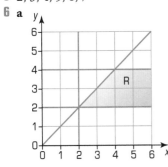

**b** $y > x$  $x > 1$  $y < 5$  **7** 22  **8 a**

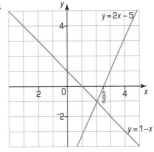

**b** $x = 2$, $y = {}^-1$

**9** 9, 10, 11, 12

**10** $^-1$, 0, 1, 2, 3, 4, 5

**11 a** $x \geqslant 6$  **b** $x \leqslant 3.5$

**12** Because square numbers have two roots, a positive and a negative one

**13** $x = {}^-1$, $y = 2$

**14** $x = \frac{1}{2}$, $y = 4$

**Exercise A9**

**1 a** £12 **b** 120 minutes **c i** 30p **ii** £7 plus 5p **d** after 30 minutes
**2** 4 km
**3 a i** 6 km per hour **ii** 6.7 km per hour **b** 6.4 km per hour
**4 a** C **b** Someone got in the bath **c** 5 minutes
**5 a** B **b** A and C show the car stopping then returning to where it started. **Actually**, the car stops when it hits the wall and does not return from there.

**Exercise S1**

**1** 48°, 32° and 18°
**2** $a = 55°$, $b = 125°$, $c = 146°$, $d = 91°$
**3** $x = 145°$, $y = 35°$
**4** $x = 15°$
**5** $x = 240°$, $y = 120°$
**6 a** $y = 26°$ **b** rhombus **c** $z = 134°$
**7** $x = 70°$
**8** Angles in a triangle add up to 180° and so:    PRQ = 180° − RPQ − PQR
                                                                                      = 180° − 35° − 90°
                                                                                      = 55°

**9** 58°

**Exercise S2**

**1 a** $y = 78°$ **b** $x = 132°$
**2 a** Angles in a triangle add up to 180°. There are five triangles in a heptagon and 5 × 180° = 900°
   **b** 540°. Angles in a triangle add up to 180°, there are three triangles in a pentagon and 3 × 180° = 540°
   **c** 1080°
**3 a** 150° **b** 30°
**4 a** make the side lengths equal **b** make all the angles 90°
**5** ABF is equilateral therefore its angles are 60°
   CDEF is rectangular therefore its angles are 90°
   Angle AFC = 90° − 60° = 30°   angle FBC = 180° − 60° = 120°
   Angles in a triangle add up to 180° so angle BCF = 180° − 120° − 30°
                                                                                      = 30° = AFC
   There are two equal angles so BCF is isosceles.
**6** Adjacent sides are equal lengths and all angles are 90°
**7** 360° − 96° = 264°. Angles in a quadrilateral add up to 360°
   Therefore 360° = 24° + 264° + QPS + QRS
   It is isosceles so QPS = QRS and 2 × QPS = 360° − 24° − 264° = 72°
                                              So QPS = 36°
**8** $x = 36°$
**9** The exterior angle of a regular octagon is 45°, but the exterior angle of an equilateral triangle is 30° so they can't fit together.

**Revision R3**

**1 a** $k = 110°$ **b** $m = 50°$
**2 a**

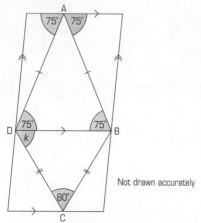

Not drawn accurately

**b** 50° **c** $x = 180° − y$ **d** $x = 180° − t − w$ or $180° − (t + w)$ **e** $180° − y = 180° − (t + w)$ so $y = t + w$
**3 a** F **b** C **c** F **d** D and or E **e** (1, 3) and (⁻3, ⁻5)

96

**4 a** (0, 8) and (2, 4) are on the line.

$$2x + y = 8$$
$$2 \times 0 + 8 = 8$$
$$2 \times 2 + 4 = 8$$

**b** $x + y = 8$

**c**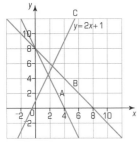

**d** $x = 1\frac{1}{2}$, $y = 4$

**5 a** $y = {}^-10$ **b** A and B

**c**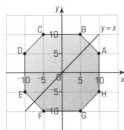

**d** $x = 0$ or $y = 0$ or $x + y = 0$ **e** $x = 35$, $y = 20$ **f** (35, 20)

**6** $x = 22.5°$

## Exercise S3

**1 a** BD$^2$ = $9^2 + 12^2$ **b** 17 cm
$$= 81 + 144$$
$$= 225 = 15^2 \text{ so BD} = 15$$

**2** 10.95 cm

**3** 14.97 m

**4** $10^2 + 24^2 = 100 + 576 = 676 = 26^2$
This means it obeys Pythagoras and so is right angled

**5** 193.13 cm

**6 a** 18.9 cm
**b** TU$^2$ + TS$^2$ = 48 + 16 = 64
SU$^2$ = 64
so STU is right angled.

**7** 5.77 km

**8** 3.87 cm

## Exercise S4

**1** 8.45 cm

**2** 74. 53°

**3 a** 124° **b** 304°

**4** 1.6°

**5** 43.60°

**6 a** $x \sin a$ **b** 41.8°

**7** 83.6° and 96.4°

**8** 45°

**9** 24.6°

**10** 37.2 m

## Exercise S5

**1** 8 cm

**2** $a = 122°$

**3** $a = 60°$

**4** XY = 4.8 cm

**5** CD = 12.5 cm

**6 a** $\frac{10}{6} = 1.667$ $\frac{14}{10} = 1.4$ $1.4 \neq 1.667$ therefore they are not similar **b** 16.67 cm

**7** Yes. They have equal angles (120° + 40° + 20° = 180°)

## Exercise S6

**1**

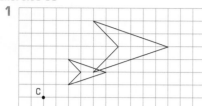

**2** scale factor = 3, centre of enlargement = (1, 4)     **3 a** 2   **b** $\frac{1}{3}$     **4** $a$ = 7.5 cm, $b$ = 55°, $c$ = 4 cm     **5** 4 or 14

## Exercise S7

**1**

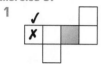

**2 A, B** and **E**     **3 a i** side 3   **ii** side 2   **iii** side 1   **b**

**4** 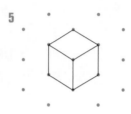     **5**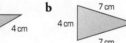

**6** 9.17 cm

## Exercise S8

These drawings show the shapes but not the exact sizes. Check your lengths using a ruler.

**1 a**   7 cm / 4 cm / 4 cm   **b** 7 cm / 4 cm / 7 cm     **2** 5 cm / 5 cm / 5 cm / 5 cm

**3 a** Right-angled triangle, base 8 cm, height 3 cm
  **b** Isosceles triangle, base 8 cm, height 3 cm, or two equal lengths of 8 cm and angle of 20.6°

**4 a** (4 cm, 6 cm right-angled triangle)     **b** 7.2 cm   **c** Actual length = 7.21 cm     **5**

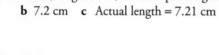

**6**

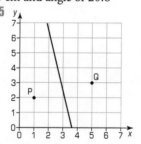

**7**

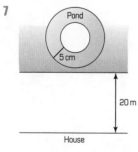

**8**

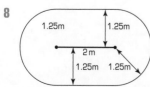

**Revision R4**

1  **a** B1: Rotate 90° clockwise
      B2: Reflect vertical
   **b** A2: Rotate 90° clockwise
      B1: Reflect vertical, and then Rotate 90° clockwise
      B2: Rotate 90° clockwise

2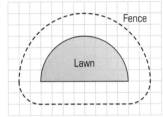

3  20.8 cm  ($\sqrt{433}$)  **b** 9.8 cm  ($\sqrt{96}$)

4

5  7.2 km  ($\sqrt{52}$)  **b** 056°  **c** 2.2 km

**Exercise S9**

1  Z X Y

2  **a** 7.2 cm  **b** 4.5 cm  **c** 6 cm

3  **a** 200 cm², 30 cm², 12 cm², 80 cm²,
   **b** 322 cm². It is equal to the combined totals of the four smaller areas.

4  **a** $p$ = 38 cm, $a$ = 65 cm²  **b** $p$ = 54 cm, $a$ = 96 cm²

5  146.16 m²

6  5744.56 cm²

7  30 000 m

8  6 cm

9  **a** 44.0 cm²  **b** 31.4 cm

10  15.6 cm²

**Exercise S10**

1  18 cm

2  75 cm²

3  A chord is a line connecting two points on a circle.
   The diameter is the largest chord as the points it connects are as far away as possible.

4  15.91 cm

5  **a** 251.33 cm  **b** 141 m

6  201 cm²

7  12.7 cm

8  8 cm

9  111.09 cm²

10  It covers 0.785 of the square    11  9    12  7.54 m²    13  84.82 cm²

14  **a** 8.38 cm²    **b** 12.19 cm

**Exercise S11**

1  142 cm²    2  108 cm²    3  625    4  **a** 74 m²  **b** 74 000 000 mm²

5  200 cm    6  235.24 cm²    7  170.65 cm²

8  3 cm and 4 cm    9  **a** 41.4 mm²  **b** 521.4 mm²

**Exercise S12**

1  105    2  48    3  120 cm³    4  4 cm

5  **a** 32 000 cm³    **b** 32 000 000 mm³

6  0.18 m³    7  **a** 240 cm³  **b** 8 cm

8  1244.07 cm³    9  120 cm³    10  **a** 828 mm³    **b** 12.08 cells

## Exercise D1

1 The sample is small and one street may not be representative of a whole area
2 Ask more than 16 people and ask people who are not her friends or in her year
3 a e.g. How often do you have your hair cut

every week    every 1–2 weeks    every 2–4 weeks    every 5–10 weeks
every 10–25 weeks    less than every 25 weeks

  b e.g. who cuts hair, age, gender, income group, hair styles cut
4 320°
5 a Pie chart angles: Hockey 135°, Rugby 150°, Football 75°.  b 32
6 a 90°  b Not possible to tell
7 a No. He could do more than one thing at the same time.  b 2 hours 24 minutes

## Exercise D2

1 a 45%  b 60

  c If there are more men working there then the proportion could represent more people.
2 a cannot be certain (as the graph only shows the trend up to 1998)

  b false (it fell by exactly $\frac{2}{3}$ from 1500 to 500)  c can't be certain (graph only for mature students)
3 a i 37.35°C  ii 38.7°C  b The temperature does not have to have a consistent change between two successive readings.
4 Somebody may have made several shorter calls that add up to more 150 minutes
5 a i 25  ii 17  b 230

## Revision R5

1 a C  b $4n + 10$  c $40 + n$  d 10
2 a No. Circumference = 1727 cm   1727 ÷ 50 = 34, so not enough room.  b 18.85 m²
3 a No. The rounding may not be exact.  b 2 h 53 mins   c Some days you don't work.
4 a $18x^3$  b 90  c 5 cm

## Exercise D3

1 95 and 101    2 7719 or 7728 or 7737 or 7746 or 7755    3 a 7  b 3    4 18
5 a total tries = $(1 \times 10) + (1 \times 3) + (2 \times 4) + (3 \times 7) + (4 \times 1) = 36$  b 2.25
6 a mean: 15 years 3 months   range: 10 months 3 days  b This pupil would have no effect on the mean and range.
7 21.8 minutes    8 73.8 cm    9 a 2 – 4  b 12  c 4.42 minutes

## Exercise D4

1 a 158 cm  b 24 cm  c 151.5 cm  d 165.5 cm    2 a median: 35   Interquartile range: 20
  b Younger and more variable age at summer fete
3 a i test A: 120 secs  test B: 100 secs  ii test A: 120 secs  test B: 70 secs
    iii test A: 60 secs  test B: 64 secs  iv test A: 51 secs  test B: 15 secs
  b Test A is better as it shows a wider spread of times  c 12

## Exercise D5

1 a i negative correlation  ii no relationship  b) No relationship for example:

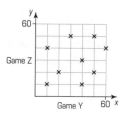

2 a The line of best fit does not have to pass through (0, 0), the origin
  b The line of best fit should pass as closely as possible to all the points
  c Lines of best fit should show the data's trend
3 a The scatter graph shows that as diameter increases so does height
  b

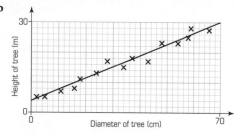

  c around 12 m
  d This is probably not a pine tree as it does not fit into the trend shown by the line of best fit
4 a The relationship shown is a negative correlation; as engine capacity increases, urban fuel capacity decreases.
  b i 31 mpg    ii 12.5 mpg    c i 3600 cm³    ii 900 cm³

**Exercise D6**

**1 a** p(yellow) $= \frac{5}{9}$  **b** 5  **c** 5  **2** She is more likely to win as 0.58 is larger than 0.5, or equal chances

**3 a** 0.11  **b** 169.1  **4** 28  **5** 18  **6** 80

**7** Disagree. He won 21% of games. This is only 1% off what the designers say he should win.

**8 a** Then the total number of sweets is 30, but 0.05 of 30 is 1.5 and 0.35 of 30 is 10.5 and you cannot have half a sweet.

  **b** Lemon: 1 Orange: 8 Cherry: 7 Strawberry: 4  **c** 120

**9 a** $0.42 \times 20 = 8.4$, but you cannot have 0.4 of a marble  **b** 50

**Exercise D7**

**1 a** RR RY RG BR BY BG  **b** $\frac{1}{6}$

**2** 2338 2383 2833 8233 8323 8332 3328 3382 3238 3832 3823 3283

**3 a** 2, 4, 8, 16, 32  **b i** $\frac{1}{9}$  **ii** $\frac{1}{3}$  **iii** $\frac{1}{3}$  **4 a i** 0.19  **ii** 0.25  **b i** 24  **ii** 60  **iii** 3

**5 a** TTT HTT THT TTH THH HTH HHT HHH  **b** 150

**6 a i** 0.0025  **ii** 0.095  **b** 80  **7 a** $\frac{9}{64}$  **b** $\frac{27}{512}$  **8 a** 0.09  **b** 36

**Exercise D8**

**1 a** Louis, as he collected the most data

  **b** No. Heads and tails appeared almost equally.  **c** 0.5023

**2 a** Richard: Purple – 0.51, White – 0.49; Pat: Purple – 0.46, White – 0.54

  **b** Purple – 0.485, White – 0.515  **c** The combined results  **d** 9700

**3 a** 0.475  **b** 190  **4 a i** 0.125  **ii** 0.40625  **b** 0.000977

**5 a** Tails, Heads. Tails  **b** 50%  **c** $\frac{1}{2}$  **d** No. The probability of getting heads is 50%

**Revision R6**

**1 a** Positive correlation: smaller horses are lighter.  **b** About 592 kg  **c** About 167 cm  **d**

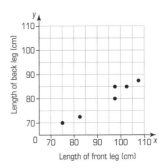

**2** A. A has $\frac{26}{65}$, B has $\frac{25}{65}$

**3 a** $9 + 34 + 72 + 24 + 25 + 6 = 170$.  **b** 2.7  **c** 38 000

**4 a** $\frac{75}{245} = \frac{15}{49}$  **b** $\frac{3}{245}$  **c** $\frac{1}{3}$

**5 a** 0.000 625  **b** 0.048 75  **c** 120

**6 a** W, L, L  **b** 45  **c** 0.6  **d**

**Practice Test Paper 1**

**1 a** 8, 25  **b** 20, 7  **c** any two of $n - 6$  $n \div 4$  $\sqrt[3]{n}$

**2 a** C. It is the most regular  **b** Same. All 27 cubes.  **c** 27  **d** $1 \times 1 \times 18$, $1 \times 2 \times 9$, $1 \times 3 \times 6$, $2 \times 3 \times 3$,

**3 a** Isosceles  **b** Yes. Opposite sides parallel.  **c** No. Angles not 90°

**4** 7, ⁻3, 4, ⁻21  **5** ⁻6, ⁻1, ⁻30  **5 a** $\frac{8 \times 3}{9 \times 4} = \frac{24}{36} = \frac{2}{3}$  **b** $\frac{2}{30} = \frac{1}{15}$

**6 a i** $x = y - 5$  **ii** $x = \frac{y}{3}$  **iii** $x = 8y + 2$  **b** $x = \frac{y}{3} - 4$ or $x = \frac{y - 12}{3}$  **7** 24 km/h

**8 a** $(x - 1)(x - 6)$  **b** $x^2 + 10x + 21$

**9 a** positive  **b**

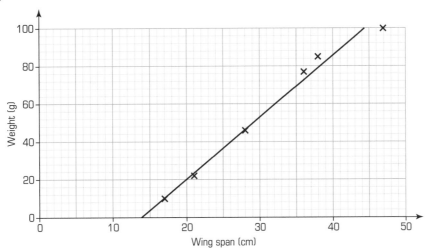

  **c** about 30 g  **d** No. The value is not near the line.

**10** $\frac{13}{16}$ 16 possibilities; 13 even  **11** orange $\frac{9}{16}$,  lime $\frac{3}{16}$, lemonade $\frac{3}{4}$

**12** Two sides add to 8. The four possible combinations are: $1 + 7$, $2 + 6$, $3 + 5$, $4 + 4$  **13 a** Thames  **b** $3 \times 10^6$

**14 a** $a = 3$  $b = 2$  **b** $c = 5$

**15 a** No. The percentage of Sei whales has risen from 19% in the original population to 27.5% in the estimated population.

  **b** 90%  **c** 75%  **d** The whale population has decreased by a large percentage.

**16 a** Greatest value = 168, Median = 150, Box is less wide than for girls, minimum value is more than 136.

**b** Other school: range is greater, interquartile range is less, median is greater.

**17** A → R, B → P, C → S, D → Q

**18** $n(n+1)(n+2)$

One number must be in the 3 times table as they are consecutive.

So the product will be divisible by 3.

**Practice Test Paper 2**

**1** 9    **2** 35%

**3 a** Three coordinates from (0, 7) (1, 6) (2, 5) (3, 4) (4, 3) (5, 2) (6, 1) (7, 0)    **b** $x + y = 7$

**c**

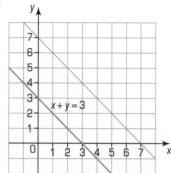

**4 a** max = 72    min = $^-$54    **b** $3 \times 4 = 12$, $4 \times {}^-3 = {}^-12$, $12 + {}^-12 = 0$

**c** 3 answered: all correct

10 answered: 6 correct, 4 incorrect

17 answered: 9 correct, 8 incorrect

**5 a** 50.3 cm$^2$    **b** 9 cm

**6 a** $\frac{9}{8} = 1.125$    **b** $x = 15$    **7 a** 15    **b** 48°    **8 a** red: 200, yellow: 250    **b** yellow: 12.5 blue, 7.5    **9** 29

**10 a** Sum of interior angles = 6 × 180°. Each interior angle = 1080° ÷ 8 = 135°    **b** 30°

**c**

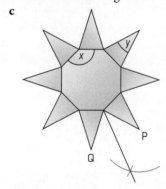

**11 a** $1 = 1^3$,    $0 = 0^3$,    $^-1 = {}^-1^3$    **b** Numbers between 0 and 1

**12 a** No: $8.6^2 + 9.4^2 \neq 13.2^2$    **b** No: cos 42° ≠ $\frac{17}{25}$

**13 a** 18 km/h    **b** 10 minutes    **c** 12 km/h

**14 a** $4x = {}^-16$    $x = {}^-4$    **b** $8x + 7 = 12x - 27$, $4x = 34$, $x = 8.5$

**15** $\frac{n+4}{3n}$    **16** 32.76%    **17** $21x - 7 = 20x$, $x = 7$    **18** 12.7 cm

**19** Interior angle of a pentagon = 108°    $n \times 108° + m \times 90° \neq 360°$ where $n$, $m$ integers

**20** AP = 7.5 cm (by Pythagoras)

BC = $\frac{BQ}{3} = \frac{PB}{PA} = \frac{12.5}{7.5}$ (similar triangles)

BQ = $\frac{3 \times 12.5}{7.5} = 5$ cm